praise for *Who Are You Following?*

"We've had the honor and privilege to stand close and watch what God is doing through Sadie, who has a trustworthy track record of wholeheartedly and contagiously following Jesus. *Who Are You Following?* is a beautiful invitation to combat the temptations within social media and culture and embrace who God has wonderfully created us to be. Put this wisdom-filled book at the top of your reading list!"

—**Louie and Shelley Giglio**, pastor of Passion City Church, cofounders of the Passion Movement

"I am so grateful for this timely and important book. In her down-to-earth, honest, transparent, vulnerable, and hilarious manner, Sadie challenges us to consider the voices that are forming and shaping us, offering wisdom and practical advice to ensure we are becoming more Christlike."

—**Christine Caine**, founder of A21 and Propel Women

"Throughout these pages Sadie's contagious love for God will penetrate you. She challenges and requires all of us not to settle for the easy way but instead to embrace the only one who will fulfill us."

—**Jennie Allen**, author of *New York Times* bestselling *Get Out of Your Head*, founder and visionary of IF:Gathering

"Sadie Robertson Huff's passion for Jesus is inspiring. If there is anyone who can balance having influence on social media with a deep love for Jesus, it's Sadie. In *Who Are You Following?* she dives deep into important truths about who we are, online and off, and how we can experience God's perfect love while trying to make a difference."

—**Craig Groeschel**, pastor of Life.Church and *New York Times* bestselling author

"Sadie Robertson Huff is a voice for our generation, and her book *Who Are You Following?* speaks directly to this moment in time. With her characteristic wit and humility, Sadie unravels for us the quagmire of social media and points us to the clarity of the cross."

—**DawnCheré Wilkerson**, pastor and cofounder of VOUS Church

"Show me who you're following, and I will tell you who you'll become. We are always following someone. In a generation where anyone can be an influencer and have a platform, we need to choose wisely those we follow.

Sadie is a voice you can trust and follow. I know this because she has chosen to use her influence and platform to help others find the freedom she herself found in Jesus. This book is filled with truths that will empower you to live the life God has purposed for you.

Here is a beautiful invitation to join a movement of people who choose to follow the only one worth following, Jesus. He is the one who knows you better than you know yourself and has a beautiful story for you to be the authentic woman you are called to be."

—**Alex Seeley**, pastor of The Belonging Co, author of *Tailor Made* and *The Opposite Life*

"Sadie is such a trusted voice, such a wise friend, such an example to many of us of how to live well and live a life near to God. Nothing has shaped my life more than those who have led me and I'm thankful that Sadie is one of those voices."

—**Annie F. Downs**, author of *New York Times* bestseller *That Sounds Fun*

"This book is a reflection of God's heart for our social media–driven world. We love Sadie and are so grateful this book exists to help people explore what it means to follow Jesus."

—**Cody Carnes & Kari Jobe Carnes**, Christian music singers and songwriters

who
are
you
following?

also by Sadie Robertson Huff

NEW YORK TIMES
BESTSELLING AUTHOR
SADIE
ROBERTSON
HUFF

who
are
you
following?

W PUBLISHING GROUP

AN IMPRINT OF THOMAS NELSON

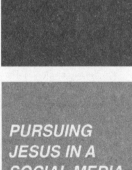

PURSUING
JESUS IN A
SOCIAL MEDIA
OBSESSED
WORLD

Who Are You Following?

© 2022 Sadie Robertson Huff

Published in Nashville, Tennessee, by W Publishing, an imprint of Thomas Nelson.

Published in association with the literary agency of United Talent Agency, LLC.

Thomas Nelson titles may be purchased in bulk for educational, business, fundraising, or sales promotional use. For information, please e-mail SpecialMarkets@ThomasNelson.com.

Any internet addresses, phone numbers, or company or product information printed in this book are offered as a resource and are not intended in any way to be or to imply an endorsement by Thomas Nelson, nor does Thomas Nelson vouch for the existence, content, or services of these sites, phone numbers, companies, or products beyond the life of this book.

Unless otherwise noted, Scripture quotations taken from The Holy Bible, New International Version®, NIV®. Copyright © 1973, 1978, 1984, 2011 by Biblica, Inc.® Used by permission of Zondervan. All rights reserved worldwide. www.Zondervan.com. The "NIV" and "New International Version" are trademarks registered in the United States Patent and Trademark Office by Biblica, Inc.®

Scripture quotations marked AMP are taken from the Amplified® Bible (AMP). Copyright © 2015 by The Lockman Foundation. Used by permission. www.lockman.org

Scripture quotations marked ESV are taken from the ESV® Bible (The Holy Bible, English Standard Version®). Copyright © 2001 by Crossway, a publishing ministry of Good News Publishers. Used by permission. All rights reserved.

Scripture quotations marked NLT are taken from the Holy Bible, New Living Translation. Copyright © 1996, 2004, 2015 by Tyndale House Foundation. Used by permission of Tyndale House Publishers, Inc., Carol Stream, Illinois 60188. All rights reserved.

Scripture quotations marked NLV are taken from the New Life Version. Copyright © 1969, 2003 by Barbour Publishing, Inc.

The Scripture quotations marked NRSV are taken from the New Revised Standard Version Bible. Copyright © 1989 National Council of the Churches of Christ in the United States of America. Used by permission. All rights reserved worldwide.

Scripture quotations marked WEB are taken from the World English Bible™. Public domain.

ISBN 978-0-7852-8991-3 (HC)
ISBN 978-0-7852-8993-7 (TP)
ISBN 978-0-7852-8994-4 (eBook)
ISBN 978-0-7852-8995-1 (audiobook)
ISBN 978-0-3106-3679-3 (custom)

Library of Congress Cataloging-in-Publication Data

Library of Congress Control Number: 2021945467

Printed in the United States of America

22 23 24 25 26   LSC   10 9 8 7 6 5 4 3 2 1

To Honey—Writing this book while pregnant with you challenged me to write with more passion, truth, and love than ever before. Your dad and I pray that you will live an abundant life, choosing daily to follow Jesus.

And to Mom, Two-Mama, Mamaw Kay, and Mamaw Jo—Thank you for showing Honey and me generations of following Jesus.

contents

foreword

PURSUING JESUS IN A SOCIAL MEDIA–OBSESSED World. Isn't that a spot-on description of one of our generation's greatest challenges?

Pursuing Jesus can be hard enough, but with roughly 4.2 billion active users on social media, the voices of our world have gotten a lot louder. With family, friends, peers, businesses, skeptics, trolls, and even the neighbor's dog filling our feeds, it's so easy to get distracted by all the noise.

Over half the global population can now be seen, heard, acknowledged, liked, disliked, celebrated, and criticized by virtually anyone, anytime, anywhere. And our attention has become a commodity. We're told to look, dress, think, talk, and act a certain way. This creates an overwhelming amount of confusion and pressure—leaving our minds full and our hearts empty.

In *Who Are You Following?* Sadie encourages you to examine your own heart as you navigate social media culture, what you post, what you watch, who you're following, and what you're ultimately seeking. She doesn't shy away from digging into the deeper motivations of our hearts, whether they're related to dating relationships or friendships or our longing for fame and acceptance.

As she mentions throughout her book, our ultimate aim is *Jesus*. Period. After all, one of His most critical commands consisted of two simple words: "Follow Me."

It wasn't an invitation based on convenience. He didn't use 280 characters or ask people to subscribe to His channel. He wasn't looking for a thumbs-up. It was a clear call to obedience.

Jesus called people to deny themselves (Luke 9:23). To "come and see" (John 1:39). To experience abundant life (10:10). To receive true rest (Matthew 11:28). To be free and forgiven (Galatians 5:1). To be used by God in greater ways than even He was (John 14:12). And to spend eternity with the King of kings (5:24).

A Follow to Jesus isn't just a tap on the screen. Following Jesus involves receiving a new identity. He—not your culture— defines who you are. He wants you to see yourself as He sees you, no more, no less. And He sees you as lovable, infinitely valuable, and fully capable through Christ.

Sadie gets this!

Over the last several years, we've had the privilege of watching God work through her life and ministry. We have been so impressed by Sadie's heart for God and for people. She is authentic and vulnerable, and she radiates God-confidence! It's clear Who she is following.

You might be picking up this book wondering, *Is this for me?*

I'm not an influencer. I don't have a ton of followers. That's okay. None of that really matters. Let us remind you that as a follower of Jesus, you don't have to be on social media to influence others. You have the ability to be an influencer every time you walk into a room. You don't need a million followers or a personal brand to impact your school, home, community, city, or workplace. You just need to be living like Jesus.

As you dive into *Who Are You Following?* our hope and prayer is that you will be encouraged by Sadie's wisdom and inspired by the gospel. Even in the midst of a noisy world, remember that Jesus' command was simple. Decide that your response will be too: follow Him.

TIM AND DEMI-LEIGH TEBOW

I resolved to know nothing while I was with you
except Jesus Christ and him crucified.

1 Corinthians 2:2

who is influencing you?

The bottom line in leadership isn't how far we advance ourselves but how far we advance others.
JOHN C. MAXWELL[1]

I HELD MY FINGER DOWN ON THE INSTAGRAM APP ON my home screen and hit the small circle in the left corner. Following my instruction, a message in bright red letters asked if I actually wanted to delete the app. An inaudible *tap* and it was gone.

It really needed to go. I was distracted by everyone else's lives and unhappy with my own. I finally became uncomfortable with wasting my time. It was like the numbing medicine had worn off, and I was tired of having a crooked smile. I was tired of the comparisons, tired of caring what other people thought, tired of caring too much about what others were doing, tired of feeling anxious, and tired of feeling like I wasn't enough while trying to make it look like I was.

My relationship with social media was like a dating relationship you stay in even though you know it is time to go. It seems like no amount of insecurity or anxiety can break the attachment and your desire to stay.

I had already removed the app multiple times, rearranging my home screen and deleting every social media app, only to go back to the app store a week later and download them all again. It was as if I was in that toxic cycle of breaking up and getting back together, hoping that when I came back, the problems that I had before would be gone. But the thing with problems is, they usually are not fixed until you work on them. I finally faced the reality that in all my deleting and redownloading, I hadn't helped any of our world's problems with social media, not even my own.

I also realized I needed to say something to social media: "It's not you; it's me." The unhealthy side of our relationship would be easy to blame on specific social media platforms, but truthfully, I knew this was not all their fault. I needed to change.

Screen Time Alert

It would be pretty naïve for us to think that social media doesn't have an impact. Let's talk statistics for a minute. Millennials (those born from 1981 to 1996) spend an average of two and a half hours per day on social media.[2] I personally know people who spend way more than that, closer to five or six hours each day. One friend even admitted to me that her screen time was seven hours a day on a certain social media app. If that's not disturbing enough, a recent study shows that teens thirteen to eighteen years old spend an average of seven and a half hours on social media *each day*.[3] These numbers are on the rise, too, as more of our culture and commerce revolves around social media.

- Eight billion live videos are viewed on Facebook every day, with about 1 billion video views on YouTube and 10 billion on Snapchat.[4]
- There are 1,074 Instagram photos uploaded every second, making it about 65,000 photos uploaded every sixty seconds.[5]
- As of March 2019, Snapchat reached 90 percent of all thirteen- to twenty-four-year-olds and 75 percent of all thirteen- to thirty-four-year-olds in the US.[6]
- Fifty-four percent of social media users research products on social media, and 71 percent of users are more likely to purchase products and services based on social media referrals.[7]

It makes me wonder: How do these numbers add up over time? Projections estimate the average adult will spend six years and eight months of their life on social media.[8] Now, can you even pretend to think that social media is not influencing your life? I am not the only one in a relationship with social media, and I'm definitely not the only one with a sometimes-unhealthy relationship.

Our prevalent social media use isn't helping us. The stats above are alarming, and so are these:

- Ninety percent of teens believe online harassment is a problem for people their age, and 63 percent identify it as a "major problem."[9]
- The Pew Research Center's 2018 survey of US teens determined that 59 percent of teenagers have experienced at least one of six different forms of abusive behavior online: name-calling (42 percent), being the subject of false rumors (32 percent), receiving unsolicited explicit images (25 percent), having their activities and whereabouts tracked by someone other than a parent (21 percent), receiving physical threats (16 percent), and "having explicit images of them shared without their consent" (7 percent).[10]
- Approximately 40 million American adults—roughly 18 percent of the population—have an anxiety disorder, according to the Anxiety and Depression Association of America.[11]
- "It's estimated that 16.2 million adults in the United States, or 6.7 percent of American adults, have had at least one major depressive episode in a given year."[12]
- "Nine percent of the US population, or 28.8 million Americans, will have an eating disorder in their lifetime."[13]
- "Ten thousand two hundred deaths each year are the direct result of an eating disorder—that's one death every 52 minutes."[14]

I know we can't blame all this on social media alone. There are studies that attribute the problems in our culture and mental health to many sources: the breakdown of the family; the increased rate of children growing up in one-parent homes; the decrease in young adults' involvement in church; the rise in people citing the desire for wealth, fame, and material things as their number one priority; and the shift in our society to live alone rather than in family groups. There are many contributing factors to the rise in anxiety and depression that we are seeing in our society today, but we can't ignore the role something is playing when we are literally spending hours on it every single day.

Yet it's not only the number of hours we spend scrolling and liking that could be a problem. An investigation that surveyed more than 1,700 young adults in the US compared the levels of anxiety and depression to the number of social media platforms used. "People who frequented higher numbers of social platforms reported higher levels of depression and anxiety."[15] Social media is continually changing, taking on new forms, with new apps being developed every day. Just when you master one, another "it" platform that "everybody's on" pops up. I think it's safe to say that anything we are spending up to seven hours a day on is worth looking at closely and considering whether it is leading us to the life we desire.

I have a large social media presence. And although my own relationship with it has been unhealthy at times, and I know there is a lot of negative and even alarming content out there, I have also seen incredible things happen through these apps that give us a chance to connect with the world.

> I THINK IT'S SAFE TO SAY THAT ANYTHING WE ARE SPENDING UP TO SEVEN HOURS A DAY ON IS WORTH LOOKING AT CLOSELY AND CONSIDERING WHETHER IT IS LEADING US TO THE LIFE WE DESIRE.

I want to see more of that positive, encouraging messaging spring up. That's why I'm writing this book. This is me doing what I can to help us all wake up to the issues caused by our obsession with our screens—interactions that often provide the wrong answers to questions we don't even know we're asking.

So wait. Don't close this book yet.

This isn't a radical movement to delete social media from every electronic device around the globe. Again, social media in and of itself is not a bad thing. It offers connection and a platform to tell a story. Our story. But because online connections are a picture of the health of our world, I wonder if we should take a step back and get honest about how we're doing.

ASK YOURSELF:

Which people or information sources are influencing your life the most right now? Are you being thoughtful about who and what you pursue?

Looking at our Gen Z and millennial generations, I wonder if we were more cautious about who we were following when we were kids than we are now—when it matters most.

I remember as a kid not being happy about being told to follow someone I didn't deem worthy of being a leader. In elementary school our class had a special role assigned each week, the job of line leader. You didn't have to do anything to get this leadership position; you just waited for your turn in alphabetical order. This meant that even the worst kid in the class was going to be the line leader at some point, which meant that you were going to have to follow him. There was even a song: "We're following the leader, the leader, the leader. We're following the leader, wherever he may go." Following the line leader really bothered me. Even then I was aware of and thinking about who I was following and whether they were leading me in the right direction.

Or maybe your teachers assigned someone to "watch the class" while they were out of the room. Wasn't it the worst when they assigned someone you knew wasn't worthy of that role? The kid who was always causing trouble when the teacher wasn't looking was suddenly the one "in charge."

As an adult I've looked in the mirror and asked myself, *Was I more bothered by who I was following and where they were taking me when I was a kid than I am now, when it matters more?* My answer? *Yes.*

Be honest with yourself. I don't think I'm the only one who would answer that question with a yes.

It's easy to follow someone during their ten minutes of

fame—the person with the biggest viral videos on TikTok, the trending "it" couple on Instagram, the reality star with the most dramatic scene of the week. Recently I heard someone say they think TikTok is the worst thing for our generation and they'd never let their own kid have it, yet they use it for their own entertainment. Don't get me wrong. There's nothing wrong with entertainment, but when we admit that this form of entertainment is "the worst thing for our generation," we must be ready to ask ourselves, "*Is this the way I should be entertaining* myself?"

> WAS I MORE BOTHERED BY WHO I WAS FOLLOWING AND WHERE THEY WERE TAKING ME WHEN I WAS A KID THAN I AM NOW, WHEN IT MATTERS MORE?

I, too, scroll through certain social media platforms more than I realize, more than I plan to. Especially when I look up and thirty minutes or an hour—time I'll never get back—is gone. But the real question is, Who do we *really* want to follow? Especially when we realize that who we are following is influencing us and the way we live our lives.

Influence's Superpower

Most of us don't even realize the power that others' influence has over us. If you've purchased something from a swipe-up link on Instagram, you've been influenced. If you've looked in the mirror and felt a little differently about your beautiful body after seeing perfect (and likely edited) bikini photos online, you've been influenced. You've been influenced if you can't figure out why you're lonely, why you're insecure, why you struggle so much with confidence, and why you're not finding the relationships you want to be in. At some point, you might even realize the power of influence when suddenly you're looking in the mirror at a stranger.

The term *influencer* is a new one. It was just added to *Merriam-Webster Collegiate Dictionary* in 2019. When social media began, it didn't take long before companies started realizing that people were actually following what others online were doing, wearing, and using. So they tapped them to advertise their products. There is nothing wrong with this; I think it just highlights a fact that we can't ignore: we are being influenced on social media. It's literally in people's job titles.

Not all social media influence is bad influence. Many of you probably heard about this book from social media. Maybe you watched a sermon online that changed your life. Maybe you met your spouse on social media! Social media is what we make it. I am merely pointing out that overall, the influence social media has had on our lives is negative. We can blame tech companies all day long, but I say *this is our problem to fix.*

The dirty little secret of social media is that we are often following people who don't have a clear direction in life and may or may not really know who they are. So how in the world could we expect them to help us find who *we* are? Those women online with seemingly perfect bodies, the people in perfect relationships, and the perfect moms with angelic children? They are struggling with the same things we are, because they are human and have the same twenty-four hours in a day that we all do. In fact, there are times people even seem to view *me* like that. I get comments on my posts that say, "It must be nice to not have problems like *xyz*." But the fact is, I totally have those everyday problems. I just don't share them on social media.

When you follow the wrong directions on a map, you end up lost. When you follow the wrong influences in your life, you will find yourself in that very same position—lost. There is no sense wasting our lives searching in all the wrong directions when there is a clear direction for all the things we desire in life.

So how do we follow the right path in life?

Matthew 7:7–8 says, "Ask and it will be given to you; seek and you will find; knock and the door will be opened to you. For everyone who asks receives; the one who seeks finds; and to the one who knocks, the door will be opened." Friend, I want you to have your own direction in life. Let's spend some time together asking, seeking, and knocking.

ASK YOURSELF:

Why are you experiencing feelings of insecurity, loneliness, emptiness, and jealousy after following so many people and trends on social media?

Welcome to Eudora

When I was sixteen years old, I was so excited to get behind the wheel. Despite some early nerves, it didn't take long before I was way too confident to be driving my friends everywhere.

Just a few months after getting my license, I said I would drive my best friend to the Friday night football game. I had no trouble on the way there because I was following Google Maps on my phone. On the way back from the game, I was pretty confident that I knew the way, so I went for it without the app's help. The drive was going smoothly for a while. I thought I was recognizing the sights and landmarks, and I was having such a good time dancing in the car with my friend that I didn't realize I'd taken a major wrong turn. About an hour and twenty minutes in, when we should have been getting close to home, we saw a sign that said Eudora, Arkansas, Post Office. And y'all, I live in *Louisiana*.

Notice I had no trouble getting to my destination with the map, but the minute I stopped paying attention and was just dancing around with no true direction, I ended up in the wrong state.

Maybe you feel the same way.

When we focus on our own ambitions, we end up with false confidence or even a fake confidence, temporary highs, and a feeling of being flat-out lost in a big world, following every trend that makes the slightest promise of a better life, a better body, and a better day, without true, soulful contentment. Each trend comes and goes, and then we are on to the next one.

My friend got in the car with me thinking I knew the way because of the confidence I showed from the driver's seat, confidence I had simply because I had a driver's license when she didn't. But the reality was, I was just as confused and clueless as she was.

Do not just assume someone is leading you in a good direction simply because they have a confidence in their walk, because they have somehow been assigned that role, or because they are famous. Not every leader is a good one. It's important that you know who you're following, not just for yourself but also for those who are following you. Why? Because whether you realize it or not, you are influencing the people in your life—be it friends or family, your children, your coworkers, or your church community. Those around you are learning from your example, even if they don't realize it.

> NOT EVERY LEADER IS A GOOD ONE. IT'S IMPORTANT THAT YOU KNOW WHO YOU'RE FOLLOWING, NOT JUST FOR YOURSELF BUT ALSO FOR THOSE WHO ARE FOLLOWING YOU.

I do consider myself a good leader, but the truth is, the best leaders are typically the best followers. If you are following me, I will be quick to tell you that I am not leading you to *me*. To be honest, that would offer you very little. Instead, I want to lead you to Jesus. Because even though I am a leader, I am first a follower. I follow Jesus.

The Ultimate Follow

Let's talk about Jesus, a leader and influencer worth following. You know, the cool thing about Jesus is that, just like social media influencers, He was not ashamed to ask you to follow Him. He was confident in where He was leading. Many people ask you to follow them today. I've seen many YouTubers unashamedly implore us to click and subscribe with lots of fun, emotive hand motions. Many influencers on social media are giving out valuable information: how to start your own business, how to train your baby to sleep (one that I'm very interested in at the moment!), how to do a full face of glam makeup in ten minutes or less.

But Jesus could confidently ask people to follow Him because He knew He was not just doling out self-help advice; He was leading His followers to life. Jesus said, "I am the way and the truth and the life. No one comes to the Father except through me" (John 14:6).

Notice something: Jesus was confident not only in where He was leading people but also in who He was. He wasn't wishy-washy, on with this trend or the next. As a matter of fact, He wasn't on trend at all. He was not constantly changing His message to try to maintain His following either. The things He was saying and doing were very countercultural. He was leading His followers to something new—something no one had seen or heard before.

We'll get to who Jesus claimed He was and what that means for you in a minute, but first we need to understand where He was leading. He said that He was leading us to the Father. You might say, "Okay, then who is the Father?" The Father is the God of the universe. He is the Creator of the world and everything in it. He is Jesus' Father and our heavenly Father.

Genesis 1:27 says that we are made in God's image with a purpose: "God created mankind in his own image, in the image of God he created them; male and female he created them." Ephesians 2:10 tells us that "we are his workmanship, created in Christ Jesus for good works, which God prepared beforehand, that we should walk in them" (ESV). Those two verses address our identity, our purpose, and our calling—some of the biggest issues of life.

Your next question might be, "What is the Father like?" Maybe you've heard He is judgmental or harsh.

The Father is love. It's not just that He is loving, which He is, but God's Word tells us that He actually *is* love. "Whoever does not love does not know God, because God is love" (1 John 4:8). He is the essence of love. His love for us is laid out so beautifully in John 3:16: "For God so loved the world that he gave his one and only Son [Jesus], that whoever believes in him shall not perish but have eternal life." God's love is seen through His act of giving up His Son, Jesus, to die in our place.

Sounds pretty radical, huh?

The crazy thing is, we're all headed toward death. It sounds bleak, I know, but it's a rare "100 percent" statistic—we're all going to die someday. The question of what happens after we die is one that we should all consider. God's Word tells us the good news that through Jesus we have the gift of eternal life! What Jesus did covers us for all eternity. He stepped into our place, which meant taking on all our sins so that we can live free of them with our holy Father God forever. God is our Creator.

He is love, and He has provided a way to His promised sin-free life after this life.

He gives us just a glimpse of how awesome it will be in Revelation 21:

> I saw "a new heaven and a new earth," for the first heaven and the first earth had passed away. . . . I heard a loud voice from the throne saying, "Look! God's dwelling place is now among the people, and he will dwell with them. They will be his people, and God himself with be with them and be their God. 'He will wipe every tear from their eyes. There will be no more death' or mourning or crying or pain, for the old order of things has passed away." (vv. 1, 3–4)

This is where Jesus is leading us.

Why am I telling you all this in a book about social media? When you first follow someone, you typically look at their profile and their page to figure out who they are and what they do. If you're going to take a good look at who you're following, and you either already follow Jesus or are considering following Him, I want you to take some time to find out who He is, what He is doing, and where He is leading you.

The Way

When I became a first-time mom, I saw for myself that there are a lot, and I mean *a lot*, of methods out there for everything.

You want to know the best way to breastfeed? There are many, *many* methods. Looking for the best way to get your baby on a sleep schedule? There are hundreds of ways. Want to know how to breathe during labor? Yup, you guessed it! There are several effective techniques! Honestly, all the options really overwhelmed me because it required me to keep asking what way was the best way. And you won't ever know until you try figuring it out yourself.

Thankfully, Jesus' language is different from the mom squad throwing out all these ideas. He didn't say, "I have a way for you to get to the Father and it's the best method on the market." No, He said, "I am the way." *Period.* There are no other options. No other shortcuts. You don't have to try a million different options for what best fits you; the cross is one-size-fits-all. Therefore, you don't have to wander lost and anxious with no purpose. You can confidently walk through life to your eternal hope because you know the way.

The Truth

Have you ever played the game Two Truths and a Lie? My brother-in-law, who is an absolutely hilarious human, has a go-to for this game. He always says, "I'm Chance, I love myself, and I'm ugly." This makes me literally laugh out loud just typing it. The joke is that the lie is he's ugly.

Sometimes it's easy to know what the truth is, and other times it's really hard, especially in a culture where truth is relative. What is actually loving? What is actually kind? What is confidence? With so many questions, you can find a different truth in every corner or culture you turn to. Yet Jesus doesn't say, "I have another idea for you to consider." He says, "I am the truth." Whatever ultimate truth you search for, you can find it through the life of Jesus.

The Life

We all have different ideas of what "the life" would be. For some it's living on a yacht in the Bahamas. Some might say it's traveling the world, building a cabin in the mountains, or never having to worry about finances. Others might say the life is simply having all your family living in the same place. All these scenarios would make life pretty fun and amazing—but they'd all go away when we die. They are only temporary.

Jesus' words "I am the life" are not meant to simply serve as a temporary comfort while you live this temporary life. Beyond this life, Jesus is your ticket to eternity. His sacrifice, made out of great love, is the only way to have eternal life and a hope of heaven. Whatever life you think would be amazing on earth is only the tiniest glimpse of what heaven will be. I don't know about y'all, but that is who I am following. And Jesus not only invites us to follow Him but also provides support for us as we do.

We have talked about the Father, we have talked about the Son, but I haven't yet mentioned the Spirit, who is basically your influencer. He is your swipe-up link, if you will. The Spirit will guide you through the night and the day. In fact, when Jesus was preparing to die on the cross and His disciples were sad that He was leaving, He said to them, "It is to your advantage that I go away; for if I do not go away, the Helper (Comforter, Advocate, Intercessor—Counselor, Strengthener, Standby) will not come to you; but if I go, I will send Him (the Holy Spirit) to you [to be in close fellowship with you]" (John 16:7 AMP).

You may wonder how Jesus, who died two thousand years ago, can be someone you follow. Well, He thought that through too. His Spirit is here to be your guide.

ASK YOURSELF:
Do you want the Spirit to be your "top influencer"? Will you open your heart to His help and wisdom throughout your day today?

How Will I Know?

With all the confusing messages and overwhelming number of swipes, clicks, links, Tweets, Snaps, and TikToks, how do I know if I'm being influenced by Jesus or influenced by the world of media? Galatians 5:22–23 says, "The fruit of the Spirit is love, joy, peace, patience, kindness, goodness, faithfulness, gentleness, self-control" (ESV). If you're following the Spirit, you can expect these things to naturally flow from your life.

People ask me all the time how I am so joyful, and the answer is that I'm following His Spirit—therefore His fruit is flowing out of my life! Before I was following the Spirit, the fruit of my life was totally different. Jesus put it this way: "Every good tree bears good fruit, but a bad tree bears bad fruit. A good tree cannot bear bad fruit, and a bad tree cannot bear good fruit" (Matthew 7:17–18).

When I was following every trend the world threw at me, following the influence of the guy I was dating, and following anything that was "cool," my life and attitude looked a lot different. During that time I was really struggling with anxiety, ending up as one of those statistics I referenced earlier. If you have read my book *Live Fearless*, you know how heavy the anxiety got. This was also when I struggled with my body image and never felt like I was good enough. Instead of the beautiful words from Galatians describing the fruit of the Spirit, I was welcoming into my life anxiety, stress, insecurity, uncertainty, and discontentment.

You may feel the exact same way.

I want you to know that I don't feel that way anymore. There is hope. I am not perfect, but I feel the fruit of Jesus in my life. I truly have joy, peace, and love dwelling within me. I don't have to filter my life or alter my caption to make it seem better than it is. I am truly happy.

I want that joy for you, and I know who can lead you there. The good news is that you're just a follow away from a different influence.

WHEN YOU'RE FOLLOWING JESUS,
YOU'LL FIND WHAT YOU'RE
REALLY LOOKING FOR: THE WAY,
THE TRUTH, AND THE LIFE.

what are you seeking?

Wisdom is learning to discern God's ways in a cluttered world of opinions, personal thoughts, mantras, and make-believe.
KEN COSTA[1]

WE WERE IN NEW YORK CITY AROUND CHRISTMASTIME for a girls' trip. It was my mom, my two sisters, and me along with my grandmother and great-grandmother. I love the city at that time of year—everything is decorated for Christmas, the tree is up in Rockefeller Center, and the streets are packed with shoppers. There we were among it all, bundled up in our winter coats and hats. Every time we'd walked into a store that was perfectly heated, we'd take off our winter gear, then later we'd bundle back up to go to the next store. When it started snowing, it felt truly magical.

We were trying on shoes in a store that had what seemed like an endless supply, when my sister Rebecca decided she wanted to go to a shop a couple stores down. Bella, who was about seven or eight at the time, asked Mom if she could go.

Mom said, "Okay, just stay with Rebecca." Of course Bella had every intention of doing so. The problem was she didn't know the name of the store she was going to or where it was. She just knew to follow Rebecca, who had on a long black coat.

Can you guess how many long black coats there are in New York City? It's like black suitcases on the airport baggage carousel. There are a lot! As my sisters were walking down the sidewalk, Bella dropped her mitten. In the seconds it took her to pick it up, she took her eyes off Rebecca, and when she looked back up, she started following someone in a long black coat again. It took her a while to realize it wasn't Rebecca, and by the time she did, she was an entire block away from our family in a sea of strangers. How quickly we can end up somewhere we never intended to go if we aren't paying close attention to who we are following!

> HOW QUICKLY WE CAN END UP SOMEWHERE WE NEVER INTENDED TO GO IF WE AREN'T PAYING CLOSE ATTENTION TO WHO WE ARE FOLLOWING!

Typically when we follow someone or something, the

hope is that doing so will lead us to what we are looking for. If I ask the grocer which aisle the bread is on, I will have no problem following him to aisle three, because I've made clear exactly what I'm looking for and I trust that he knows where to find it. Google Maps guides us to the place we want to go only because we've typed the address into the search bar. But the world of social media is different. Perhaps we've forgotten the first step of following someone or something: determining where we want to go.

We're trapped in a world where the end result isn't necessarily what we're looking for; we're basically all about random, blind following and a whole lot of clicks.

Let's think back to that grocery store. What if we went there to pick up a few items to fill our pantry, but when we walked through those electric doors we started following the person who had the best style? Then someone else caught our attention, and we went down the aisle they were on. It is highly unlikely that we would leave the grocery store with what we actually came for. And most likely we would spend way more time at the store than we'd planned. We'd then have to go back to a still-empty pantry, or we'd begin to fill it with things we didn't need or even want to begin with.

Often we don't intend to see the things we see, think about the things we end up thinking about, spend the hours we spend, or even buy the things we buy. We just weren't paying attention to who we were following. The problem is, we don't know who we are, what we want, or where we are going. We might have had a vague idea, but we weren't intentional about following the people who knew how to get us there, or we got distracted and forgot what we wanted in the first place.

Behold the Lamb of God

In the Bible Jesus' disciples knew exactly who they were looking for, and when they found Him, they stopped "scrolling" and dropped everything to follow Him. That seems like a wild concept: to be able to just drop your plans in life and follow someone you have never met. But many of us do that all the time without even realizing it. We follow people on social media that we have never met and will most likely never meet, and we begin to change things about ourselves without even realizing we are doing it.

It might not happen overnight, but in time you will start to look like who you follow. You can't help it. The first time I saw bike shorts, I looked at a friend and said, "I'll never wear those." It's now two years later, and I have three pairs. Have you ever noticed how friend groups all start looking alike? It's incredible how fast a trend can take hold.

Many of these things are just silly, like fashions, dance moves, or even phrases that come and go, so what's the worry? We may not be really changing our lives, but this shifting of our values—the things that we once said we would never do and now find ourselves doing—can happen on a deeper level. Maybe it was a thought shift from caring about who God says you are to caring more about who people say you are. Or maybe it was a priority shift from putting others first to only caring about yourself and doing what makes you the happiest. We are all being moved and shaped by the people we follow in much more important things: our beliefs, our morals, our values.

Now, back to the disciples. Let's read John 1:35–41 to understand why they decided to follow Jesus the moment they saw Him.

John was standing with two of his disciples, and he looked at Jesus as he walked by and said, "Behold, the Lamb of God!" The two disciples heard him say this, and they *followed* Jesus. Jesus turned and saw them following and said to them, *"What are you seeking?"* And they said to him, "Rabbi" (which means Teacher), "where are you staying?" He said to them, "Come and you will see." So they came and saw where he was staying, and they stayed with him that day, for it was about the tenth hour. One of the two who heard John speak and *followed* Jesus was Andrew, Simon Peter's brother. He first found his own brother Simon and said to him, *"We have found the Messiah."* (ESV, emphasis added)

A little backstory so that we can understand the gravity of this moment: For hundreds of years there were prophecies that a Messiah was coming. At this point in history, John the Baptist had been out in the wilderness preaching about the coming Messiah. There were many people who believed and were waiting for the prophecies to be fulfilled. So on this day, when they heard John say that Jesus was the one they'd been waiting for, they asked Jesus where He was staying and immediately followed Him.

Now that you know the context, you can understand why, when Jesus asked them, "What are you seeking?" they didn't answer with, "We don't know." Instead, they said, "We have found the Messiah." They'd finally found what they were looking for. So they dropped everything they were doing and began to follow Him wherever He was going.

> WE NEED TO BE MORE INTENTIONAL ABOUT WHAT WE ARE LOOKING FOR SO THAT WE CAN BE INTENTIONAL ABOUT WHO WE BEGIN TO FOLLOW.

I love how immediately after gaining this following, Jesus turned and asked, "What are you seeking?" He gave them a moment to reflect on their intentions. He sought to make sure that they weren't just aimlessly following someone because they heard it was cool or because they just thought He seemed legit. They were able to commit to following Him because He was who they were looking for, and they knew He was leading in the direction they wanted to go.

We need to be more intentional about what we are looking for so that we can be intentional about who we begin to follow. This is true not just on social media but also in our real-life relationships, including future friends, spouses, mentors, or work associates. If you do not know what you're looking for in a future spouse, you will end up in situations you never imagined yourself in. If you don't know the kind of person you want to be friends with, you may join friend groups that lead you away from your desired version of yourself. If you don't know the job you want, you may sign up for whatever opportunity comes your way, even if it's not helping you move toward your goals. The disciples set the best example for us because they knew what they wanted and where they wanted to go—and so the second they saw Jesus, they dropped everything else and started following Him.

ASK YOURSELF:

What are you looking for in life? What are you wanting out of the relationships you are in? Are you looking in the right places?

Matthew 6:33 says, "Seek first the kingdom of God and his righteousness, and all these things will be added to you" (esv). Notice that the verse does not just say to seek the kingdom, but to seek the kingdom *first*. Many of us may have Jesus on our list of things we are following, but if we are honest, He is nowhere near first place in our searching, and then we wonder why we don't experience the goodness of His love and the life that He has for us. We want the blessing of Jesus, but we don't want the commitment of following Him. This verse tells us all these things will be added to us if we seek Him first. So it's as simple as can be: if you seek God, you will find the things of God. Whatever you seek you are going to find, so the question of "What are you seeking?" might be the most important one to answer.

The Seven Times Factor

Have you seen the Netflix documentary *The Social Dilemma*? In it, the actual programmers, coders, and masterminds behind social media platforms explain that they created these systems with constantly improving algorithms to give us more and more of what we seek. What you're looking for, you're going to find, because the creators of these programs will literally set your algorithm to make sure that you do.

I haven't even watched *The Bachelor* this past season, but after one quick Instagram search to see what everybody was talking about, my Explore page was full of *Bachelor* accounts and posts for weeks. You would have thought I was Bachelor Nation in the flesh if you saw my Explore page.

Or maybe you searched for a pair of tennis shoes but decided not to buy them. The next day, how many ads did you see of that same pair of tennis shoes that you resisted buying the night before? If you seek it, they will make sure you find it! (And how many times do we cave and end up with those shoes on our doorstep?)

There is an interesting cardinal rule in advertising that's called "The Seven Times Factor." This states that potential customers need to see an ad seven times before they make a purchase. The more times you see a product advertised, the more likely you are to buy it. You can translate that to other parts of life as well: the more often you are presented with a thought or an idea, the more readily you will accept it. Scary, right? Our ideas, thoughts, habits, morals, values, likes, and dislikes are being shaped simply by repetition, and that all goes back to who we are following.

Whatever you choose to look at constantly, you invite into your world—and you'll keep seeing it every single day. If you're looking at workout videos, you're always going to have people in sports bras and spandex shorts on your feed, killing it and crushing it. If you're looking for inappropriate pictures, it's going to be in your face on every social media account. And once something is seen, it is very hard to unsee.

I used to have a Snapchat account but ended up deleting it because it was not good for my mind. The magazines that the app had inside of it became an unnecessary temptation and distraction for me. The articles on Snapchat's home page were always about the latest drama between so-and-so, the hottest body challenge, photos of people posing nearly naked, the top ten sex positions, and gossip on who slept with who. And, because of the time I was spending on the app, guess what I started to think about? Other people's drama, my body, and sex. As a senior in high school, I'd never struggled with lust before, but all of a sudden I was having thoughts I'd never had. It made me think about things that I did not need trapped in my eighteen-year-old mind.

James 1:14–15 says, "Each person is tempted when he is lured and enticed by his own desire. Then desire when it has conceived gives birth to sin, and sin when it is fully grown brings forth death" (ESV). It is important that we stop ourselves at an early point of temptation, because those fleshly desires can lead us down a really bad path. Had I not deleted Snapchat during that time, I might have ended up in some dark places.

> YOU CONTROL THE MESSAGES AND THE PHOTOS THAT COME INTO YOUR WORLD AND INFLUENCE YOU.

You may be in the same boat. We have to be careful what we seek out, because what we seek is what we'll find, and *what we find is going to influence our lives.*

I want you to know that, ultimately, you control the messages and the photos that come into your world and influence you. The more you allow yourself to be negatively influenced—be it inappropriate imagery or something that makes you feel insecure—the more those influences will feed into who you are becoming. Although it is hard to unsee something, it is not hard to delete or unfollow. You have the power to stop following whatever might be leading you down a bad path.

ASK YOURSELF:

How are you being passive or intentional about the influences on your thought life?

Guard Your Heart

I always pick a word for the year, which I learn about and meditate on. This year it's *pure*, which is defined as "free of any contamination; without any extraneous and unnecessary elements."[2] If you want to be pure, you can't add unnecessary or impure elements. It's about stripping all that away and working on the pure essence of who you are.

Purity can seem like a hard thing to maintain in a high-content world, but Psalm 119:9 gives us a way to accomplish it. "How can a young man keep his way pure? By guarding it according to your word" (ESV). We guard our purity by refusing to conform to the world and sticking with God's ways. As Romans 12:2 says, "Do not be conformed to this world, but be transformed by the renewal of your mind, that by testing you may discern what is the will of God, what is good and acceptable and perfect" (ESV). Purity requires refinement. Refinement is not easy, but it is necessary for becoming the person you desire to be.

When I deleted Snapchat it felt like a big deal because everyone had it, but you know what? I have not missed out on anything. In fact, I believe that because of my choice, I am a better person with a freer and purer mind. I did not want to continue conforming to the pattern of the world when that pattern was unhealthy for me. I am not saying that it is unhealthy for everyone, but it is very important to be aware of the effects Snapchat (or any other social media platform) has on you and to be willing to get rid of things that are dragging you down a bad path. My husband, Christian, had also deleted the app about a year before we met because of the easy and secret access it gave to inappropriate images. I am so thankful that he also took the leap to not conform to the pattern of the world just because it is the pattern of the world. We both wanted to transform our minds so that we no longer were enslaved to a thought pattern that was not healthy. We wanted God's good and perfect will for our lives.

I remember someone asking us, "If y'all didn't have Snapchat when y'all started dating, how did y'all see each other?" First off, this made me laugh, because we literally just saw each other in real life as much as possible. That's what dating is all about—spending real time together learning about each other, not just sending hundreds of selfies throughout the day. We also had Facetime for when we were a long distance apart and spent a lot of time talking on the phone.

> THERE ARE WAYS TO LIVE A LIFE THAT DON'T STEAL FROM WHO YOU ARE.

There are ways to live a life that don't steal from who you are. The only way to find them is to know what you are searching for and to stop following anyone that doesn't take you there. Unfortunately, the more you seek the people or things that take you to places you don't want to go, the quicker you will find yourself there. There is no shortage of material available on social media for every style, temptation, and walk of life. Seek out what inspires you to be better, look for the people who point you to the life that you want through Jesus, and unfollow, block, or delete all the rest.

I've kept a very strict account of what I allow to influence me. First off, I simply delete an app if it is not beneficial to my mental health, and I frequently take a break from certain apps. I don't scroll Instagram's Explore page; I stick to who I personally follow in my feed. I unfollow or mute people when they post things that I don't need to be seeing. There's no benefit to my life to keep following and keep feeling like I'm not enough.

I hardly watch TV anymore unless it is a game show, a sweet series that is appropriate, or a family-friendly competition show. I am careful with the music I listen to. Even if a song is very popular or a video has gone viral, if I know it is something I do not want stuck in my head, I just do not listen. I guard my heart.

> THERE'S NO BENEFIT TO MY LIFE TO KEEP FOLLOWING AND KEEP FEELING LIKE I'M NOT ENOUGH.

Proverbs 4:23 says, "Watch over your heart with all diligence, for from it flow the springs of life" (AMP). I know that what goes in is what flows out. You may think my life seems uptight or boring because of how limited I choose to be with what I see, hear, and read, but honestly, I have a super fun life because I have a free mind and a healthy heart.

I didn't always have this disciplined approach. I used to

watch every popular TV show and movie, follow all the cool people, have every app, and learn every word to the latest songs. And I can honestly say I have a much more fun and joy-filled life now than I did back then. I joined TikTok for a bit because that seemed like what everyone was doing, and it was actually really fun for a minute. I ended up deleting it from my phone for a time, though, because I soon found out that app in particular takes you down roads you don't even ask to go on. As soon as you finish one video another pops up, and you don't even have to follow someone to see their video. The lack of control over what I was putting in my heart and mind through that app caused me to quickly realize it wasn't for me. Every now and then I get back on to post a fun video, but I am careful with what I look at and how much time I spend on it. I know it's not the way to the life I'm looking for.

ASK YOURSELF:

When have you noticed some kind of media having a negative impact on your feelings and mental health? What changes could you try making to protect yourself from that kind of negative impact?

Proverbs 4:24–27 goes on to say, "Keep your mouth free of perversity; keep corrupt talk far from your lips. Let your eyes look straight ahead; fix your gaze directly before you. Give careful thought to the paths for your feet and be steadfast in all your ways. Do not turn to the right or the left; keep your foot from evil." These are wise words, words that pretty much cover everything we do: your mouth (the things you say), your eyes (the things you look at), your feet (the places you go). But it all starts with your heart, with what you put in and what flows out. It's difficult to guard your heart when you are mindlessly scrolling the popular page or watching whatever pops up on TikTok or YouTube.

I can tell you with certainty that I have way more fun now than I did when I consumed all that media. Back then I was struggling with fear, insecurity, and worldly thoughts. Unfortunately, at that time in my life I had not clearly defined what I was seeking, so every follow, every scroll, every like led me to places I never intended to go. I have worked hard to get healthy in these areas and now I am very aware of how I'm feeling as I scroll or as I watch movies or shows. I take immediate action if something isn't sitting right. I have walked out of plenty of movies, and I've never once regretted the peace I felt that night as I fell asleep.

I'm not saying to get off screens entirely. Actually, there are great things to watch, follow, and listen to, and lots of positive ways to interact! It just takes a little more intentionality. Are you ready to step into the amazing life you were created to live? Then don't waste your time mindlessly watching, scrolling, and searching. Be intentional with your choices and what you are looking for. Let's not get complacent about the things that we see and put into our hearts and minds.

Jesus offers us an abundant life. The alternative is so much less than what we were created for.

Jesus is the way, the truth, and the life. He is the way to an abundant life. So stop following everything else for pieces of what Jesus can give you in whole. Seek Him and all these things will be added. We need hope in this world of chaos; we need peace, love, joy, and purpose; we need a Savior. We need the Messiah. We need Jesus. And behold, He has already come and He is ready for you to seek Him.

What are you seeking? I hope that you are seeking the One who offers you the abundant life here and now and, even more, a hope that extends to eternity.

PROTECT YOURSELF FROM MESSAGES AND IMAGES YOUR HEART DOESN'T NEED. ASK FOR WISDOM AND STRENGTH TO SEEK WHAT IT DOES NEED.

how do you go from liked to loved?

To be loved but not known is comforting but superficial. To be known and not loved is our greatest fear. But to be fully known and truly loved is, well, a lot like being loved by God. It is what we need more than anything. It liberates us from pretense, humbles us out of our self-righteousness, and fortifies us for any difficulty life can throw at us.

TIMOTHY KELLER[1]

WHEN CHRISTIAN AND I FIRST STARTED DATING, WE talked casually for a while, and after we got to know each other more, we started to really like each other. We also started telling each other that we liked each other. If you have ever been in that place in life when someone tells you that they like you, then you know it is the giddiest moment ever. The "I like you" phase is full of nerves and excitement, and it's bursting with possibility. You feel all the feels.

Although it's exciting to be liked, it's also intimidating. You quickly become aware that the relationship could end at any moment because there's not much commitment involved with it. It's still so fragile, and it can seem like one wrong move could change everything. Your relationship is pretty much based on good times, small talks, a lot of flirting, and physical attraction.

> WANTING TO BE LIKED USUALLY MEANS PUTTING PRESSURE ON YOURSELF TO PERFORM AND BE A VERSION OF YOU THAT SOMEONE ELSE CHOOSES. IT DOES NOT NECESSARILY GIVE YOU THE FREEDOM TO BE FULLY YOU.

In those early days I felt so much pressure. Christian wasn't putting any pressure on me; I was putting it on myself, not wanting to do or say something that could end our relationship. I think some of that stemmed from past relationships not working out. I wanted to stay likable—whatever that meant in that situation. Wanting to be liked usually means putting pressure on yourself to perform and be a version of you that someone else chooses. It does not necessarily give you the freedom to be fully you.

Bringing Your A Game

The official definition of *liked* includes these words: to be "agreeable, enjoyable, or satisfactory."[2] But the social media definition of liked is to win one's approval. For me, the pressure came from wanting to be agreeable, to seem enjoyable, and to bring Christian satisfaction. I wanted to "win his approval," and winning means bringing your best.

I was bringing out my A game for Christian. I was getting spray tans, having my nails done, borrowing friends' clothes, and even practicing the dance moves that I would do in the car when he picked me up to go on a date. I wish I was kidding about that last part, but no, I was full-on choreographing my moves and crafting my playlist to make sure I could crush the car ride on our date. All the while just trying to be likable.

As I look back on this time, I realize that I did not just go through these feelings in dating relationships; I lived my life like this. I would leave a conversation and think about the words I'd said over and over, questioning if I'd said everything right. I would walk out of a room and wonder what everyone thought of the way I looked.

And as far as social media went, there were several pictures I never posted because I knew they wouldn't get the likes that another one would. I even remember years ago deleting pictures on social media that did not get as many likes as the other ones— not because I didn't like the picture that I'd posted, but because of my craving to maintain a certain number of likes. I didn't realize at the time how I was constantly obsessing over people liking

> THE DESIRE TO BE RELEVANT CAN BE JUST AS HARMFUL AS THE DESIRE TO BE LIKED; BOTH CAN CAUSE YOU TO QUESTION WHO YOU ARE AND PUSH YOU TO DO THINGS YOU'RE NOT OKAY WITH.

me. Only later was I able to see the self-doubt, fear, and insecurity that I walked in.

This is embarrassing to admit, but there were times I watched TV shows I didn't even enjoy just so I could quote from them later and sound relevant among friends. That sounds pretty pathetic, but I doubt I am the only one who has done that. Or times I would wrestle with wearing a certain outfit that was so not me just because it was the trend. The desire to be relevant can be just as harmful as the desire to be liked; both can cause you to question who you are and push you to do things you're not okay with.

ASK YOURSELF:

When have you recently said or done something solely out of a desire to be liked? When have you made choices that express your real self?

Don't Take Yourself Out of the Game

When Christian and I became boyfriend and girlfriend, I took on another role in addition to girlfriend: FBI Investigator Sadie

Rob. Everything was great between us, and then I had the idea that I needed to look at my boyfriend's Instagram. Well, not just look at it—investigate it.

I'd seen Christian's Instagram so many times. But when I became Investigator Sadie, I started noticing stuff that I'd never really cared about before, including the girl that he went to a date party with, who was really pretty. All of a sudden I had a different perspective as I looked at those photos. I noticed her in a different way. I'm not even in college, and she's in college, and Christian is in college; they have way more in common. My mind went through every other thought that you could possibly have while comparing yourself to somebody.

And then I saw another girl that he went to a party with, and I thought she was pretty too. I spiraled as I thought about how much fun they must have had and how beautiful those girls were, with their blonde hair and blue eyes, having fun at date parties.

After my investigation I walked away concluding I was no longer good enough for the relationship. I figured I should do everybody a favor and exit. I'd save Christian the hassle. I went to Christian and started telling him how I was feeling and processing all of my discouraged thoughts out loud. And then I realized that I had done this exact thing a few times in the past.

Years earlier I'd been dating a guy, and somebody said something about my looks not being up to par compared to another girl who had previously dated him. That really stuck with me—I carried that message into so many relationships that followed. But I couldn't see that for a long time, and it got in the way of me getting close to people. It wasn't that others weren't willing to love me; it was that I didn't feel very lovable. It wasn't that they weren't willing to date me; it was that I didn't feel good enough to date them.

That little lie had been planted in my heart years beforehand, and I almost let that hateful message affect my relationship with the person I would later marry.

I caught myself in the middle of running away from Christian (when he hadn't done anything wrong). He was standing there willing to give me his love, pursuing me with love and respect. He didn't love me any less in that moment; I just felt less lovable. I felt like I was not good enough to accept his love.

Christian shared with me something very powerful that day. He said, "Yeah, those girls were indeed attractive girls." At first it felt pretty odd to hear those words coming out of my boyfriend's mouth, but then he said, "However, I am captivated by you." He went on to say, "You can notice something is attractive, because the fact is, it's attractive. But to be *captivated* means that you hold all my attention." That day I stopped investigating and rested in the security that he was captivated by me.

We need to be that way with Jesus—to be captivated by Him. Yes, other people's lives might be attractive to us. They may even seem better than ours. But instead of letting our perspective make us feel less than, we need to be captivated by the fact that God in and of Himself is enough for us in any season. We have to stop getting distracted by all that we see and let God hold our full attention.

So many times we do this with God. He is loving us, pursuing us, and asking us to be in a relationship with Him. He has written a couple-thousand-page love letter to us, but we have to allow ourselves to be loved.

We must begin to take God at His word that we are loved. When we refuse to allow ourselves to feel loved, we stop a relationship from being able to grow. Just like I was doing. But once we can accept His love into our hearts, we can trust His Word and His calling for our lives, no matter what that might look like measured up to another. Be captivated by your Creator, and don't lose sight of His gaze.

ASK YOURSELF:

How can you put yourself in a position to be captivated by the God of love today?

The Like Button

I think a huge part of why we struggle with the need to stay relevant and liked is because our social media–obsessed culture literally revolves around the Like button. There are lots of articles about the actual mental damage the Like button is causing us, but despite threats to get rid of it, it's not going anywhere. A *TIME* magazine article called "Why Instagram Is the Worst Social Media for Mental Health" reported alarming statistics found in the #StatusOfMind survey published by the United Kingdom's Royal Society for Public Health. It explored how multiple social media platforms foster "a 'compare and despair' attitude" and how Instagram in particular has a negative impact on anxiety. People feel lonely, not good enough, as if they need to perform, and yet they are obsessed with the idea of being and staying liked.[3]

The Like button on social media mimics acceptance, such as someone giving you a compliment or agreeing with you in conversation. It feels good to be seen and validated. So good, in fact, that we keep going back to it over and over. PBS News Hour reported that "our social reward system activates the ventral striatum, a part of the brain that focuses on decision making and reward-related behavior. It's the same area that's fired up when people gamble, enjoy a slice of cake or have sex."[4] It may sound extreme to consider the physiological effects of social media, which seems so innocuous, but the effects are being widely studied and reported on.

As a society we are addicted to social media, to seeing who likes our posts and liking others' posts, but it doesn't hold real meaning in our lives. (And trust me, when I say "we," I mean me too.) Social media is addicting because it is set up to be addicting.

As I was researching this, I realized that social media tends to bring on a lot of insecurity, self-doubt, and anxiety, which are the same feelings you may have in the "I like you" phase of relationships. One study that looked at social media usage in more than sixty-five hundred adolescents found that those who spent more than three hours per day using social media may be at increased risk for mental health problems (including anxiety, depression, suicidal thoughts, negative self-image, and loneliness).[5]

The irony of the double tap is that while the Like button has trained us to be likable, it has prevented us from feeling truly loved. We post our curated lives and edit our true feelings and struggles to maximize the rewards. Another study looking at the connection between social media and mental health stated, "Those who are adept at creating perfect images of themselves, or their lives, can also endure anxiety and fear rejection based on what they see online. They may even question if their friends genuinely like their 'real' personal lives if their personalities don't align with what they present online."[6] The desire to be liked in such a way that we filter who we truly are is moving us away from feeling loved because it is making it impossible for us to be truly known.

A Fearless Journey to Unconditional Love

The Bible says something shocking in 1 John 4:18: "Perfect love casts out fear" (ESV). This blows me away because of the amount of fear I've experienced in relationships. Yet here we read that it is actually love that gets rid of fear. Unlike striving to be liked, perfect love is when you are fully known, and because it is God's love, it is never-ending.

Tim Keller said it best: "To be loved but not known is comforting but superficial. To be known and not loved is our greatest fear. But to be fully known and truly loved is, well, a lot like being loved by God. It is what we need more than anything. It liberates us from pretense, humbles us out of our self-righteousness, and fortifies us for any difficulty life can throw at us."[7]

You don't have to fear that this love will leave when it sees you on your bad days and knows your deep secrets. Even when you're not likable, you're loved. Instead of the insecurity triggered by the likes, or lack thereof, perfect love brings complete security because it does not change based on how much you change.

Early in my relationship with Christian, there were several times I thought he was going to tell me that he loved me. Like the time we were sitting on the beach and the sunset was perfect and he gazed into my eyes—you know, when the scene was set perfectly, the likable moments. But Christian did not say those words then. Nor did he say them when we were dancing under the stars together. Nope. Those words were reserved.

When Christian told me he loved me it was the day after the most vulnerable talk that we'd ever had. We'd shared our life stories, and it was not always agreeable, enjoyable, and likable, but it was real. It was who we really were and what we had really been through. For the first time in my relationship with Christian, I felt known and loved. It was only after he knew me—the good, the bad, the imperfect, the reality—that he could love me and that I could truly feel loved by him.

When we hide who we really are and stay simply likable, we make it hard for someone to love us—and if they do, we find it nearly impossible to believe them. We still live in that fear mentality of, *What if they found out this?* or *What if they saw the way I react on hard days?* Or maybe it is more of a social media mindset: *If I don't photoshop my pictures, they won't find my body desirable*, or *If I don't keep up this image, I'll lose my followers.*

If this is you, I want to say this in the most loving way I can: The most this mentality will ever get you is temporary highs from moments of being liked. The insecurity it brings, however, will be long-lasting.

Christian and I have taught each other a lot about the difference between being liked and being loved. The difference between them is being known. Our wedding song was "Known" by Tauren Wells, and if you haven't listened to it, I cannot recommend it highly enough. I love how the song talks about being known and loved; it points to some of the most important aspects of my relationships with God and with Christian, and the way I view my daughter.

Being known is the key to getting rid of fear in a relationship. Before that night of open, real sharing with Christian, I had been living to present my most likable self. Once I dropped that front, he could see the real me. After I learned this lesson, I started applying it in all my relationships. Instead of continuing to exchange the true version of me for the likable version of me, I allowed my true self to shine past whatever insecurities I felt. I would rather be loved for who I am than liked for who I seem to be in the right light.

It is not just in romantic relationships that we need to allow ourselves to be known; being known will benefit your life in every setting. You will do a better job in your work if you do not have the fear of pretending to be someone you aren't. You will have a

49

> I WOULD RATHER BE LOVED FOR WHO I AM THAN LIKED FOR WHO I SEEM TO BE IN THE RIGHT LIGHT.

stronger relationship with your family if you share with them more about your life. You will have more meaningful friendships if you open up about what is really going on with you. I think one of the keys to my own spiritual growth has been sharing some of the personal things that I have gone through with people who truly know me so that they can speak into my life with wisdom and truth. Being known opens the door to a life of depth.

ASK YOURSELF:
Are you sharing your true self with others so that you can be loved for who you are, not just liked for who you seem to be?

Not Just Seen but Known

The journey to being loved comes through being known. When we keep up the façade, when we present the best, filtered versions of ourselves, we prevent others from really knowing who we are. We are *seen* but not *known*.

Being seen is the cheapest version of being known; visibility will not fill your heart or nourish your spirit. People want so badly to be seen when their true desire is to be known. Trust me, you could be seen by millions and feel like the loneliest person. Yet you could be known by just a few and feel totally secure. I hit a million followers very quickly after going public on Instagram during my time on *Dancing with the Stars*. But while my Instagram following was growing, I was losing my closest circle of friends. That was one of the loneliest and most painful times of my life.

In 2014 I was invited to go on the show. It was a big opportunity and one that thrust me into the spotlight like I had never been before. Up until then, I felt like the attention wasn't really on me; it was on my family. By the end of my eleven weeks on the show—when I placed runner-up—my life had changed so much, even though I didn't feel like I had changed at all.

I was excited to get back to my life at home and my friends, but when I got back to school, the first thing one of the girls said to me was, "We don't want to hear about it, so don't even mention it." She was referring to my experience in LA on *Dancing with the Stars*. Obviously, I did not mention it after she said that! She clearly wasn't lying, either, because I don't remember my group of friends ever talking about it or asking me any questions about it. I stopped getting invited to things. I got booted from our lunch table. They probably assumed none of it bothered me because I had all these followers and fame. But all of that fame meant nothing to me when I felt invisible to the ones I really cared about. A hundred thousand likes on a picture does nothing for you when you have no one to hang out with. To the outside world I had everything, but inside I was missing something I greatly desired—friendship. Never assume you know what someone is going through just because you have seen where they've been.

Followers Do Not Equal Friendship

A follower can know only so much about you, and that's how it should be. A follower sees you, but just enough to give you a double-tap heart. Meanwhile, your friends actually know your heart. A follower can see your highlight reel, but a friend walks with you in the highs and lows. A follower can unfollow you and you don't ever have to know, but when a friend walks away, it is the most painful experience. I have millions of followers on Instagram, but I certainly don't have millions of fans or anywhere close to millions of friends. What matters to me is friends. The people I can call, who pick me up when I've fallen or I'm down, and who I can do the same thing for.

ASK YOURSELF:
Are you living your life in a way that attracts followers or true friendship? How can you check in on people's hearts today, not just check in on their feeds?

If you're seeking true friendship, true understanding, and true support, don't be fooled by those who like you for what you are doing for them, for the way you look, for providing them with just the right content, or for how popular you are. If you don't let the opinions of others stop you from going for what God has put in your heart to do, you will look back and be shocked at how far you go. Just don't base success on the number of people following behind; base it on the amount of purpose you are fulfilling in your heart.

The Whole Truth

There is a woman in the Bible who tried to get away with being a hidden follower. She didn't want to be seen and didn't even consider being liked because of who everyone knew her to be. This woman is the one who had been bleeding for twelve years. I often go back to her story in Mark 5 because it shows us the kind of relationship Jesus wants to have with us.

Her health had been failing her for so long, and no doctor had been able to help her; she'd exhausted all of her options. She was known as the woman with the issue of blood, and in her culture, that meant she was not welcome anywhere.

Then one day she heard that Jesus was coming into town, and the Bible says that she thought to herself, "If I just touch his clothes, I will be healed" (Mark 5:28). As she snuck through the crowd, not wanting to be noticed, she reached out and touched Jesus, and the bleeding immediately stopped.

Right after she touched Him, Jesus stopped and asked, "Who touched my clothes?" (v. 30), unwilling to let her go as just a hidden follower. His disciples wondered why He asked, because the truth was, everyone in the crowd was touching Him. Jesus continued to look around, and the "the woman, knowing what had happened to her, came and fell at his feet and, trembling with fear, told him the whole truth" (v. 33).

Let's stop right here. She told him the whole truth. In this moment she went from being hidden to being seen, and then to being known. Jesus looked at her and, for the first time in the Bible, He referred to someone as "daughter." He said, "Daughter, your faith has healed you. Go in peace and be freed from your suffering" (v. 34).

In that moment He gave this woman a new identity in front of a whole crowd—or better said, He just affirmed who she already was. He did not see her the way everyone else did, focusing on the things that she was going through. In those days when women were on their periods they were seen as unclean for seven days. Yet this woman did not stop bleeding for twelve years. If anyone touched her, they were also considered unclean, so she was breaking the law by being in that crowd and reaching out to touch Jesus.

But He did not see her as unclean or even criticize her for breaking the law. He saw beyond her pain to who she truly was. He healed her and sent her away in peace, fully known and fully loved. This shows that Jesus' relationship with us is greater than religion, more than just a set of rules. It reaches beyond our having to be perfect. It isn't bound by our own ability.

Religion is about what we can do for Jesus, but His relationship with us is rooted in what He has already done for us. The law in Leviticus called the woman unclean, but with the new covenant Jesus called her "daughter." Jesus had the compassion to stop and connect with this woman, even when other people were waiting on Him and expecting Him to be in a hurry. He truly cared that this woman was healed.

Jesus does not want you to be another hidden follower in the crowd, striving just to be enough in life. He is so much more personable than that. He cares for you as the individual you are—flaws, imperfections, doubts, and all—and He is interested in knowing your whole story. You do not have to reach some level of perfection or likability for Jesus to acknowledge you. He already acknowledges you because He loves you with an unending love.

Experience True Love

I love the story of the woman in Mark 5 because it also shows the power of possibility when you put yourself out there. She had to press past the crowd who was judging her. She had to reach out to touch Jesus' garment. If you have a desire to be loved and known, press past that discomfort you feel and the temptation that arises to remain likable so you can *touch the garment of Jesus and experience true love.*

Social media is not the only place that creates an unhealthy view of maintaining likes. Religion, the system of striving for God's love, sadly can create the same problem. Religion might make you think you have to do something to obtain God's love, but a true relationship with Jesus says you already have God's love. Remember, "God so loved the world that he gave his one and only Son" (John 3:16). God did not say He waited for you to be so enjoyable, agreeable, and attractive in order for Him to love you and send His Son to save you. He said He already loves you so much that He willingly dove into a relationship with you.

HE ALREADY LOVES YOU SO MUCH THAT HE WILLINGLY DOVE INTO A RELATIONSHIP WITH YOU.

Society might make you feel pressure to perform a certain way to be liked by Jesus—but don't let society have the final word in your heart. The cross proves that Jesus' love is already established for you.

WE ALL WANT TO BE LOVED, BUT
THE LIKE BUTTON HAS TRAINED
US HOW TO BE LIKED. BEING
LOVED AND BEING LIKED ARE TWO
COMPLETELY DIFFERENT THINGS.

who are you comparing yourself to?

When we compare ourselves or compete with one another, it works against what God intends for us. We are designed for relationship—to be interdependent and supported by each other. We are truly better together.

CHRISTINE CAINE[1]

MY MAKEUP WAS FLAWLESS, HAIR PERFECT. I WAS wearing a beautiful gown and high heels, about to walk the runway in New York Fashion Week—and I was probably the most insecure I'd ever felt in my life. Not long before then, I'd been at a photoshoot for the Sherri Hill line of dresses that had my name on them, and the photographer had said to me, "If you would lose ten pounds, you'd look like a real model."

So on this day at Fashion Week I felt like a fake. I looked around at all the "real models" as I ate M&M's from the food table in the dressing room. I quickly realized no one else was eating. They had their black coffee, and it seemed like that food table was just for looks, with an invisible Do Not Touch sign that everyone but me could see. My dress was a size 2 (how messed up is it that I was told I needed to lose weight when I was a size 2?!) while the other models' dresses had to be taken in even in a size 0. My dress was the only one they did not have to alter to a smaller size, yet I was the one who felt the need to alter myself to look better. Perfection is just so unrelatable, and honestly it is quite an illusion.

I can tell you from personal experience that it doesn't matter how far in life you go or what achievements you attain—even walking the runway of New York Fashion Week—you can still hold on to insecurity from things spoken over you or things you speak over yourself. I looked around at those beautiful girls and am ashamed to say that comparison crept in. I caught myself noticing not only the flaws in me but the flaws in them. I took note of who had bad skin, crooked teeth, or thin hair.

Comparison is never pretty and can easily lead to criticism. We're so in tune with our own flaws and insecurities, and then we fixate on others' flaws in order to feel better about ourselves. But I want you to know something important I've learned: you can become confident in who you are without having to tear down someone else in your mind.

You might be shocked to read about my struggles. You might think that walking in New York Fashion Week was the moment I felt most beautiful. But I will tell you again, confidence does not come from comparison, it does not come from a platform, and it does not even come from compliments. It comes from the One who made us.

I've known for years that I am fearfully and wonderfully made. I grew up with the nickname The Original and pasted Bible verses in my bathroom about confidence. I even got to live the life most girls dreamed of. But ultimately, it doesn't matter what privileges, successes, or positive experiences you've had. What really matters is where your security comes from, and it has to come from something bigger than yourself. Take it from me: if you keep on looking around you and comparing yourself to others, you'll keep on feeling insecure.

> WHAT REALLY MATTERS IS WHERE YOUR SECURITY COMES FROM, AND IT HAS TO COME FROM SOMETHING BIGGER THAN YOURSELF.

Since the Beginning of Time

I think there's no question that social media is amplifying the comparison problem. Comparison, however, has been around since the beginning of time. Cain and Abel, the very first brothers we read about in the Bible, tell a tragic story of comparison that ended in murder. Cain was so jealous of Abel because God was pleased with Abel's offering that he killed Abel (Genesis 4).

Then, not too many pages later, Abraham's wife Sarah was so jealous of the slave Hagar's ability to conceive a child by Abraham that she treated Hagar harshly—so Hagar fled to the wilderness (Genesis 16).

King Saul was jealous of David because the people said, "Saul has killed his thousands, and David his ten thousands" (1 Samuel 18:7 NLV). This is kind of like someone in 2020 saying, "This guy has a thousand views on TikTok and that guy has millions." As Saul kept stewing in his anger, "a bad spirit sent from God came upon [him] with power. He acted like a crazy man in his house, while David was playing the harp. Saul had a spear in his hand, and he threw the spear, thinking, 'I will nail David to the wall.' But David jumped out of his way twice" (vv. 10–11 NLV). You probably have never thrown a spear at someone, but you may have thrown invisible darts with your eyes when the spirit of jealousy took over.

I have a verse for you I bet you haven't put in your Instagram bio: "Do not take your wife's sister as a rival wife and have sexual relations with her while your wife is living" (Leviticus 18:18). It is believed that this verse and law was written because of the story of Rachel and Leah from the book of Genesis in the Old Testament. Leah and Rachel found themselves in major competition for a man's attention, both of them feeling stuck in an unfulfilling relationship.

Long story short, Jacob worked for seven years to marry

Rachel, whom he loved and thought was beautiful. But on the day of the wedding, Rachel's father, Laban, manipulated the situation to make her sister, Leah, Jacob's wife instead. The problem was, Jacob did not find Leah beautiful nor did he love Leah like he loved Rachel. We can see that he definitely had true love for Rachel because he was willing to go through so much to marry her. It went beyond her looks or more superficial qualities. He worked for seven years, and then, when he was tricked into marrying Leah, he was willing to work *another* seven years to marry Rachel.

In the meantime, God saw that Leah was less loved than Rachel and gave her children. Genesis is clear about Leah's hopes as she had her children. She said, "Now my husband will love me"; after a couple more babies, "Now this time my husband will be attached to me" (29:32, 34 ESV). She was always thinking that if she had just one more child, then maybe her husband would love her. She faced a constant battle of finding her worth in what Jacob thought of her.

We may not find ourselves in this exact scenario, but I believe many of us have felt this way. Have you ever thought, *If I could filter my pictures better to look like* _____, *then maybe he will love me?* Or wondered, *If I had this work done to follow the new trend in* _____, *then maybe they will see me?* Perhaps you've considered, *If I got the promotion at work that would put me on the same level as* _____, *then people would acknowledge me.* Or, *If I had a large following on social media like* _____, *then I would know that people like me.*

Too often we find our worth in what people think about us

and in how we line up with others, and we spend a lot of time and energy wondering how we can better ourselves enough for people to like us. We think that if we just do this or look like that, all our problems will be solved. But thinking this way moves us away from experiencing love. Why? Because we're moving away from who we truly are. It's like we've said before: we have to be known to be loved.

Let's go back to the love triangle in Genesis. Rachel had Jacob's love and affection—but still, she was deeply unhappy. She hadn't had any children, and she compared herself to Leah, who had her own brood. "When Rachel saw that she was not bearing Jacob any children, she became jealous of her sister. So she said to Jacob, 'Give me children, or I'll die!'" (Genesis 30:1).

That sounds pretty dramatic, right?

But let's be real—we get dramatic, too, when it comes to comparison and not having what someone else has or what we think will fulfill us. *If I don't get that or if I don't look like her, then I'm worth nothing.* We've all had a similar thought process. Allowing others to dictate our value can steal so much from our lives.

> YOU COULD HAVE LOVE AND NOT EXPERIENCE LOVE BECAUSE OF THE INSECURITY IN YOUR HEART.

Here are a few examples of how this tends to play out:

You could *have* love and not *experience* love because of the insecurity in your heart.

64

You could *have* beauty and never *feel* beautiful because of the insecurity in your heart.

You could *have* everything and *experience* nothing because of the insecurity in your heart.

Looking back, there have been many times in my life when I had what I *thought* I needed, but I felt empty because it wasn't what I truly needed.

I did not need to be skinnier to know that I was beautiful. I needed to trust that God made me how I am for a reason.

I did not need to be in a relationship to not feel lonely. I needed to believe that God was with me.

I did not need comments from people to know that I was liked. I needed to know that God loved me despite what I had been through.

ASK YOURSELF:

What does insecurity in your heart keep you from experiencing or feeling? If there are some things you think you need in life right now (for example, to lose weight, get married, receive compliments), how might growing closer to God meet a truer, deeper need in your heart?

It didn't matter that Rachel was more beautiful, and it didn't matter that Leah had more children, because they were comparing themselves to each other, causing them both to feel inferior.

You will always feel inferior when you compare yourself to someone else because you are not them. You can get all the things that you thought would provide the confidence you're looking for and still be insecure, because security will never come from temporary things or having what someone else has.

The Bible tells us of Jacob's response to Rachel's complaining about not having children: "Jacob became angry with her and said, 'Am I in the place of God, who has kept you from having children?'" (Genesis 30:2).

I want us to ask that question of ourselves: "Am I so desperate for likes, attention, praise, and glory that I'm trying to take the place of God in my own life?"

Jacob was acknowledging that Rachel's ability to have children wasn't in his control. Obviously it wasn't in Rachel's control either. So many times we compare ourselves to others about things that aren't in our control. All the while they're in God's capable hands. If we can remember that, we can rest in that. We can humbly accept that only He is God.

Maybe you're not putting yourself in the place of God, but what about your boyfriend or husband? A girl you follow on social media, or someone at your job or church? The Bible says we are supposed to be imitators of the Word, but when we put people in the place of God, we become imitators of these people. When you're confident in the Creator, you'll be confident in the creation. God must be the only one on the throne and remain on the throne.

Going back to the story of Leah, when she birthed her fourth child, Judah, she finally said, "*This* time I will praise the Lord"

(Genesis 29:35, emphasis added). And when she did, everything changed. She took her eyes off Jacob and Rachel, no longer focusing on what she did *not* have. Instead she saw the blessing God had given her.

We find in Scripture that Judah is in the lineage of Jesus. So it's no coincidence that when Leah birthed Judah and praised God, she birthed security and love. Then we go on to read that God saw Rachel's heart and intervened to give her a child, whom she named Joseph. Joseph went on to do incredible things and remained secure in who God created him to be. So the two times in these sisters' lives that God was in His rightful place on the throne, it resulted in security and love. When you stop and praise God, everything changes. You breathe confidence. You're freed up to celebrate people for who they are and the things God is doing.

Celebrating others doesn't take away from what you're doing. I acknowledge I have a high-profile calling where I'm in front of thousands of people talking about God's message.

> WHEN YOU STOP AND PRAISE GOD, EVERYTHING CHANGES. YOU BREATHE CONFIDENCE.

For too long I lived my life trying to downplay what God had for me to do because I didn't want the person I was dating or my friends to feel intimidated or get jealous. I knew Christian was different from anyone else I had dated when he looked at me and said, "Never apologize for what God is doing in your life. If it is a win for God and a win for the kingdom, then it will always be a win for me."

But here is the thing: If we are Christians, we have to understand that we are on the same team. Those words he spoke to me should apply to everyone.

Christine Caine puts it like this: "When we compare ourselves or compete with one another, it works against what God intends for us. We are designed for relationship—to be interdependent and supported by each other. We are truly better together."[2] If someone else gets a cool opportunity, you don't have to feel inferior. You have a choice. You can be jealous, or you can choose to celebrate and ask God what He has for you. When you view life as you being on a team with those who are building the kingdom, you can accomplish so much more together.

But What About John?

There was a time in my life when God was evidently doing so much. Prayers I had prayed for years were finally being answered in ministry. Things I'd asked for were right in front of me, and the only explanation was the hand of God. Other things I thought I might deal with forever, like self-doubt and insecurity, I finally felt were resolved. God was just so tangibly near, and my life was changing for the better.

During that same time someone who worked for me, who was also a close friend, got an opportunity to move somewhere new and would no longer work for me. She decided to take that opportunity because it was best for her family, which I understood. Nonetheless I'd thought we would work together forever, and I thought she was a part of the plan that God would accomplish through Live Original, the ministry I founded and am currently running with my amazing team. It was really sad for me knowing she would be going away, and it made me suddenly question God about what He was doing in her life and why she had to go, because it really hurt me.

The questioning and not understanding why this had to happen spiraled in my brain for weeks as the transition was happening. I did not even realize that I had gotten so distracted by what God was doing in her life that I'd stopped focusing on what God was doing in my own. Because I didn't see it coming when she left, I knew God clearly had a plan for her, but what was His plan for me and for Live Original? When I started focusing on her life more than my own, I quickly forgot about all the amazing things He was doing right before my eyes.

One of Jesus' disciples, Peter, did something kind of like this once. He had a super important conversation with Jesus, one where he confirmed his love for Jesus and commitment to Him, and Jesus alluded to how mightily Peter would be used in God's kingdom. Jesus literally was showing up in Peter's life in such a huge way. But in the blink of an eye, something else caught Peter's attention—well, actually, *someone* else—and it totally threw off his focus.

"Peter turned and saw the disciple whom Jesus loved following them . . . When Peter saw him, he said to Jesus, 'Lord, what about this man?' Jesus said to him, 'If it is my will that he remain until I come, what is that to you? You follow me!'" (John 21:20–22 ESV).

When John stepped into Peter's line of sight, Peter asked, "Hey, what about John?" Jesus was doing something for Peter right there in that moment, but Peter was missing it because he was too distracted by what Jesus was planning on doing for John. I can clearly relate!

Jesus' response was basically, "Stop looking at John. I am talking to *you*."

So many times we do the same thing. Jesus is trying to connect with us while we are scrolling on social media and worrying, or looking around at the other people in our life and wondering, complaining, and even commenting the second we perceive that someone else's life looks better. Are we getting so distracted by everyone else's lives that we are missing our own?

> ARE WE GETTING SO DISTRACTED BY EVERYONE ELSE'S LIVES THAT WE ARE MISSING OUR OWN?

We often miss what God is doing for us right now because we're turning and looking at what He's doing for everybody else. Now, that "turning and looking" might look different for everyone. For some, it might be thinking about how someone else's outcomes or life experiences compare to theirs. For others it might be counting Instagram likes or followers. Or maybe it's turning to the past and comparing present circumstances to a different time in life.

Instead of getting distracted, consider where God has you now. He is speaking something to your heart and building your testimony, just as He is doing for others

> DON'T LOSE SIGHT OF JESUS BY FOCUSING ON THE BACK OF SOMEONE ELSE'S HEAD.

around you. Don't lose sight of Jesus by focusing on the back of someone else's head.

Put Your Blinders On

Romans 8:35 says, "Who shall separate us from the love of Christ? Shall tribulation, or distress, or persecution, or famine, or nakedness, or danger, or sword?" (ESV). The Word of God says that nothing can separate you from the love of God, but the one thing that will make you feel separated from His love is your own perspective.

Do you know that one of the few parts of the body that does not get its oxygen from the bloodstream is the cornea, the eye's outermost lens?[3] It is like a window that controls and focuses the entry of light into the eye. Interestingly, it "contributes between 65 and 75 percent of the eye's total focusing power."[4] The cornea gets its oxygen from the air and can experience injury or infection, which can cause scars that distort your vision.[5]

Now, think how this is a picture of what we've been talking

about: nothing can separate you from the love that you have received by the blood of Jesus—except your own perspective. You can form your opinion based on the outside world, but remember it is susceptible to damage, and the scars life has brought you can affect your view of the Light.

Peter eventually did turn his focus back to Jesus, and God used him to *start the church*. John went on to do amazing ministry as well. They both wrote a couple of books in the New Testament. It is amazing what happens when you stop looking and commenting on other peoples' lives and focus on living your own.

I always say to my team at Live Original that each of us is like a racehorse. I encourage everyone to put their blinders on and not look to the left or to the right, just to run their own race. If you start looking at the others running alongside you, you'll lose your footing. You might stumble and even fall.

When I first started preaching, I struggled with seeds of doubt. I saw all the amazing pastors and speakers who gave these beautiful, eloquent sermons. I wondered what I could possibly bring to the table that would compare to them. My mom looked at me and said, "God isn't calling you to be Christine Caine or Beth Moore. He's called you to be Sadie Robertson, and He needs you to go up there and be you." She encouraged me to *learn from them but not try to be them*. God is not calling you to be anyone else but you. Learn from others and be humble, but at the end of the day, be you.

First Corinthians 12 is all about the value of every person

and every gift in the kingdom of God. The people of Corinth must have been struggling with comparison for Paul to devote a large part of this letter to this topic. He wrote, "There are different kinds of gifts, but the same Spirit distributes them. There are different kinds of service, but the same Lord. There are different kinds of working, but in all of them and in everyone it is the same God at work" (vv. 4–6). Paul described different spiritual gifts, then said, "All these are the work of one and the same Spirit, and he distributes them to each one, just as he determines" (v. 11).

Just as He determines.

Let's take a break and think about that. Who are we to question the gifts that God has given us or has chosen to give to someone else? Do we actually think He might have misjudged who should have certain abilities or roles? This is the perfect Creator God, the One who designed the whole universe and gives us life every day! We can trust that whatever He does is good and right.

Paul had more to say on this topic, so dive back into 1 Corinthians 12 with me for a minute:

If the foot should say, "Because I am not a hand, I do not belong to the body," it would not for that reason stop being part of the body. And if the ear should say, "Because I am not an eye, I do not belong to the body," it would not for that reason stop being part of the body. If the whole body were an eye, where would the sense of hearing be? If the whole body were an ear, where would the sense of smell be? But in fact God has placed the parts in the body, every one of them, just as he wanted them to be. If they were all one part, where would the body be? As it is there are many parts, but one body. The eye cannot say to the hand, "I don't need you!" And the head cannot say to the feet, "I don't need you!" . . . If one part suffers, every part suffers with it; if one part is honored, every part rejoices with it. Now you are the body of Christ, and each one of you is a part of it. (vv. 15–21, 26–27)

I think Paul made a clear case that we need to stop comparing ourselves to others and start being grateful for the unique way God created each of us. Our gifts and talents and the way we are made is His design and for His purpose. We should celebrate our differences! After all, it's our differences that come together to make the beautiful body of Christ.

Lessons from Motherhood

There is so much pressure around motherhood, and social media is such a force for comparative and competitive parenting. There are moms on Instagram sharing their whole perfect day with their children—from animal-shaped pancakes in the morning to a beautiful nature walk in the afternoon, to an educational sensory activity before bedtime in their beautifully decorated bedrooms. There are reports of how quickly their bodies bounced back and the details of their workout plan. They even tell you about how much milk they are producing and show the organized milk bottles in the freezer.

It is so easy to compare yourself when you see what everyone else around you is doing, especially when they seem to be killing it.

The other day my mom shared with my sisters and me that she didn't go through quite this level of comparison because her generation didn't see the everyday lives of other moms like we do today, where people document every perfectly cooked meal and new achievement of their children. My mom said the only thing you could really go off of was which mom wore heels to church and which mom looked like she barely got out the door!

We certainly are living in a new day when we have to be confident in who we are and the job we are doing as we're able to see what everyone else (even around the world!) is doing. These other moms sharing their lives are not doing anything wrong, but if we just believe what their perfectly curated feeds tell us, we will never feel like we're enough. We shouldn't be basing our value on how we're doing better than other people anyway. We need to base it on knowing we're doing the best we can through knowledge of who we are through God's Word.

What does the Word say about us? David wrote this in Psalm 139: "You formed my inward parts; you knitted me together in my mother's womb. I praise you, for I am fearfully and wonderfully made. Wonderful are your works; my soul knows it very well. My frame was not hidden from you, when I was being made in secret, intricately woven in the depths of the earth" (vv. 13–15 ESV).

ASK YOURSELF:

Do you believe that God formed you? Do you believe that He knit you together?

I'm going to let you in on something that might free you: You don't have to be just like that seemingly perfect person on social media. You were not created to be copied. Because God does not make copies.

I don't care if you swipe up on every single one of her stories, shop through every single makeup link that she puts out there, and literally do everything she posts about—you're never going to be her because you're not meant to be. You weren't created to be her.

She's just so pretty. She's just so skinny. She's so curvy. She has beautiful hair. She has blue eyes. Yes, she does, because that's how God created her. But it's not a bad thing that you don't have her attributes. The sooner you realize it is a beautiful thing to be you and not her, the sooner you'll live in freedom. You can't live in the fullness of her. You can only live in the fullness of you.

Wonderfully Made

Toward the end of my pregnancy, I had an ultrasound and I loved looking at the pictures from it. I'd try to make out my baby girl's cute little features and imagine what it would be like to hold her. I had left the pictures out at my parents' house, and my mom put them in my Bible to make sure I did not forget them. I threw it in my backpack and went on with my day. Later, when I opened my Bible and I saw the ultrasound pictures, I felt inspired to read Psalm 139 again, this time specifically thinking of my sweet baby. I was reading these words and staring at her little nose and her little lips. Verses 13 and 14 especially hit me a little differently: "You knitted me together in my mother's womb. I praise you, for I am fearfully and wonderfully made" (ESV).

My soul knows this is truth for my daughter. What an incredible honor it is for Christian and me to get to join God in creating life. There never has been and never will be another human being exactly like her. She is one of a kind from her little nose and dimples to her sweet little personality, created with purpose.

I look at her, and I don't compare her to a single thing. She is perfect. It is so easy to believe this verse for her because I've been a part of the way He created her. Why is it so hard for me to believe that for myself?

ASK YOURSELF:

Do the words that you speak over yourself align with the belief that you're wonderfully made? Do the actions that you take every day align with the belief that you are wonderfully made?

When I was that baby girl in my mom's womb, she wouldn't have compared me to a single thing. My mom was probably blown away by the revelation that God knit me together. It was so easy for her to praise God for her fearfully and wonderfully created child.

Yet somewhere along the way, I stopped believing that for myself. I stopped believing that I was wonderfully made as I looked in the mirror and, instead, I picked parts of myself I wished looked better. I could tell you that I wonder why I stopped believing that about myself—but I know without a doubt why I did. I compared myself to everyone and every picture of beauty, and I thought they were all simply better.

I hate that it is so hard to believe this for myself and yet so easy to believe it for my daughter. It proves that I have lost a beautiful sense of purity that I once had as a child, and I want that back.

I'm reminded, however, of something I've mentioned before: purity requires refinement. I cannot expect my mindset to suddenly go back to my childlike self just because I long for it. I have to refine my mind and change my thought patterns to be different from the ones that tore me down. I have to shield my mind from toxic thoughts. I have to speak positive words about how I was created. I have to praise God for the way my body can function and what it can produce. I have to eat well and nourish the body that I have been given. I need to be kind to myself just like I am to anyone else.

Perhaps God will help me understand these things in time as I seek Him. Meanwhile, I'm going to keep coming back to Psalm 139 and listen to Him tell me that He designed me in a way that pleased Him and that is purposed to live right now. That is so powerful in and of itself. I am fearfully and wonderfully made.

God, help my soul know that full well.

DON'T COMPARE YOURSELF
TO ANYONE ELSE. LIVE WITH
THE CONFIDENCE THAT
YOU HAVE BEEN FEARFULLY
AND WONDERFULLY
MADE, NOT COPIED.

why do you want to be famous?

Fame is a four-letter word; like tape or zoom or face or pain or life or love, what ultimately matters is what we do with it.
MR. ROGERS[1]

I AM A BIG FAN OF ICE CREAM, AND I HAPPENED TO marry a man who might just be an even bigger fan. Each night the question is not, "Are we going to get ice cream tonight?" The question really is, "Where are we going to get ice cream tonight?" It has been a big deal that our small town recently got a Baskin-Robbins. The line was literally at least an hour's wait for the first month after they opened, and Christian and I would wait it out almost nightly to get our chocolate milkshakes.

When we finally got to the window that first night, we

started to see all the workers inside noticing who we were. Everyone was running around and seemed a little intimidated to come to the window until Miss Jasmine walked up, opened the window, and with the sweetest Indian accent said, "These guys are saying that you are famous. Are you famous?" To this day she is our friend, and every time she sees us at Baskin-Robbins, she welcomes us as Mr. Christian and Mrs. Sandy (she still has no idea who I am, and I guess she misheard me from the start), and she gets our order ready.

I have always loved the quote by Mr. Rogers that I started the chapter with: "Fame is a four-letter word; like tape or zoom or face or pain or life or love, what ultimately matters is what we do with it." Mainly because people absolutely obsess over fame, but at the end of the day fame is just a word and an idea.

A Fame-Hungry Generation

The obsession with fame is nothing new. For decades people have been fawning over celebrities (have you seen video clips of the craziness surrounding the Beatles back in the day?), placing an unbelievable amount of value on the celebrity status. For years people have been striving to gain some of that status for themselves, trying to make their mark and make their name known.

A Pew Research Center study once found that many eighteen- to twenty-five-year-olds said their desire for fame was the first or second most important life goal.[2] But it's not just young people who long for the attention. A *New York Times* article called "The Fame Motive" discussed survey reports that suggested people were obsessed with fame. The research showed that "30 percent of adults report regularly daydreaming about being famous, and more than 40 percent expect to enjoy some passing dose of fame . . . at some point in life."[3] These were studies from 2006 and 2007; I can only imagine how much higher those numbers would be today, now that social media has the potential to make anyone and everyone "famous."

Here's how one recent study shows our generation's desire for fame: One out of nine millennials would rather be famous than get married. One in ten would rather be famous than get a college degree. And, the most extreme, a few even said they would disown their own family if it meant they would become famous.[4] That is desire to the *extreme*; that's desperation for fame.

It turns out that the more we use social media, the more important fame becomes to us, according to a recent UCLA study.[5] Before social media, to become famous you had to excel in your field: sports, music, acting, or something else. You had to stand out as really good at something. That usually took time and a lot of

> I WONDER IF THE ENTICEMENT OF THIS QUICK ROAD TO FAME IS STIFLING OUR GROWTH. MAYBE WE'RE NOT AS WILLING TO WORK HARD BECAUSE WE DREAM THAT FAME MIGHT HAPPEN FOR US IN AN INSTANT.

work. Today, you can build a following through social media in various ways, sometimes simply through one post going viral. I wonder if the enticement of this quick road to fame is stifling our growth. Maybe we're not as willing to work hard because we dream that fame might happen for us in an instant.

Why do we want to be famous so badly? Probably lots of reasons, but I think it's usually about gaining a sense of acceptance and validation. We're living in a lonely, disconnected time when we spend more hours connecting through our phones than interacting with others face-to-face. People are looking for reassurance that they matter, that they're doing it right, that they're seen.

The *New York Times* asked one twenty-six-year-old woman why she believes fame is such a driving force for people her age, and she said, "To be noticed, to be wanted, to be loved, to walk into a place and have others care about what you're doing, even what you had for lunch that day: that's what people want, in my opinion."[6]

> THEY ARE ON A SEARCH FOR POTENTIALLY FIFTEEN SECONDS OF PRAISE AND SATISFACTION INSTEAD OF LIFELONG COMMITMENTS THAT BRING TRUE SATISFACTION.

I would have to agree with her. We do want those things, and to be honest, I don't think those are bad things that we crave. The problem comes when a generation of people are hoping that all their deep soul desires will be met through the emptiness of fame. They are distracted from their purpose as they reach for the fame they think will satisfy their deepest longings. They are searching for the love they would experience in marriage and the security they would have in family, believing that fame could be a replacement for all of that. They are on a search for potentially fifteen seconds of praise and satisfaction instead of lifelong commitments that bring true satisfaction.

ASK YOURSELF:

Do you believe that you would be more lovable or valuable if you had a fan base?

Little *g* Gods

The obsession with fame is causing fans to create gods out of humans. We have to fix the system so this can change.

We're all human. When God created mankind, He did not make some in His image and others not. He created us all in His image and likeness. It's not good for you to make gods out of humans and to think less of yourself than others, and it's not healthy for famous people to be isolated, examined, and exalted in that way. It sets them up to fail and it sets you up to be disappointed. There's one God, and there is one way that you're going to find the contentment, validation, and joy that you seek—through Him and no one else.

When the Bible refers to God as the Creator in the Old Testament, it uses the Hebrew word *bara*, which means He is the original Creator, and He's worthy of the glory of His creation, because He created it. That word was never used for humans in the Bible, because even though humans can create things, God is *the* Creator.[7]

I've heard people describe themselves in their jobs nowadays as creators. Writers, artists, people in entertainment. There is nothing wrong with that—I believe that we are made in God's image, and we were made to create as well.

But this can get twisted in our minds. If you're creating things to share with the world and putting stuff out that people are praising, then people can begin worshiping and idolizing both your work *and* you. It's not a leap for that worship to get in your head, and you can end up with this sense of entitlement, like, *I should be worshiped for this because I created it.*

That is a problem I see in our celebrity culture. We make people feel like they're God and we treat them like a god because of the things they create. But we would not have the ability to create had God not created our brains, our lungs, our hands, and our hearts in the first place. We are not meant to be worshiped. God is. This is why our calling is not to seek fame but to seek our purpose within God's kingdom. When we do this, we may accidentally find fame. We may not. But it won't matter because we will be living our purpose.

> OUR CALLING IS NOT TO SEEK FAME BUT TO SEEK OUR PURPOSE WITHIN GOD'S KINGDOM.

Seeking Purpose

One of the top questions I get asked is, "How do I find my purpose?" In fact, I get asked this question so often that I wrote a devotional book on this topic. It's called *Live on Purpose*. I learned in writing the book that we are all genuinely seeking purpose in life.

I recently heard the term *purpose anxiety*, which is defined as "the negative emotions experienced in direct relation to the search for purpose."[8] It's the anxiety we feel when we are struggling either to find or to act on our purpose in life. Finding your purpose can mean understanding your role and value within your community, your church, or the larger world. We want to know that we matter, that what we do matters to the world and to the people around us.

Anxiety has been discussed and studied for quite some time, but the term *purpose anxiety* is more recent. Psychologist Larissa Rainey from the University of Pennsylvania studied this phenomenon, and her findings show that purpose anxiety can encompass a range of negative emotions including stress, worry, frustration, and fear as well as anxiety. Surprisingly—or maybe not that surprising because we all can probably relate—91 percent of participants reported experiencing purpose anxiety at some point.[9] So if you ever feel like you might be experiencing purpose anxiety, know that you are not alone!

Purpose is a big deal. It combines something meaningful personally and something important to the world beyond ourselves. When we know our purpose, we are more optimistic; we have hope that what we are doing means something. Understanding our purpose brings more satisfaction to our lives and even more positive interactions with our friends and family. Studies have even found that having a sense of purpose has led to better physical health and longer life expectancy.[10]

Knowing that we have purpose in life is vitally important, so it's understandable that there is some anxiety associated with finding it. The unfortunate thing is that we are looking in all the wrong places. We use different coping mechanisms to deal with this anxiety, and diving into our phones is a popular one. We freak out because we can't find our purpose, so we numb those scary thoughts with mindless scrolling, which only makes us freak out more as we see other people supposedly fulfilling their purpose. Two of the five signs of purpose anxiety come from "feeling 'not good enough' or like a failure" and "negative comparisons," which are both huge factors in depression and anxiety caused by social media.[11]

Purpose is central to our happiness, our sense of well-being, and our relationships. Without purpose, we have no direction. We ask ourselves: *Where do I find my purpose?*

> I THINK GOD GAVE EVERYONE A PURPOSE TO LOVE GOD AND LOVE PEOPLE. SIMPLE AS THAT.

Here's a hint: it's already in your heart. God doesn't leave you hanging. You don't have to wait for your purpose to arrive. Don't search the world around you for the clues; look inside. Your purpose is not some treasure hunt that only God has the map to, some prize that you have to walk around aimlessly to find. You were born with purpose and your purpose comes into play at every stage of the journey. It's a matter of tuning out the noise and pressures of the world to tune in to His message.

I think God gave everyone a purpose to love God and love people. Simple as that. A man who the Bible tells us was an expert in the law asked Jesus, "'Of all the commandments, which is the most important?' 'The most important one,' answered Jesus, 'is this: "Hear, O Israel: The Lord our God, the Lord is one. Love the Lord your God with all your heart and with all your soul and with all your mind and with all your strength." The second is this: "Love your neighbor as yourself." There is no commandment greater than these'" (Mark 12:28–31).

If you have made the decision to follow Jesus, you can easily find a window into your purpose in what Jesus tells us is most important: love God and love people. We are created to do those two things first and foremost; everything else flows from there.

ASK YOURSELF:

What have been the moments in your life when you have felt that you were living with purpose?

I think your *calling* is specific to the thing you do. Your *purpose*, on the other hand, is something you were born with and that you have in every season, no matter what you are called to.

God opens the path for you to become a teacher, a news anchor, or a doctor by giving you the gifts and abilities that you need for those tasks, but you can find your purpose in those two greatest commandments—loving God and loving people—no matter what your calling looks like. We live that abundant life Jesus promises by simply starting with those.

We never have to struggle in that purpose anxiety and ask ourselves, *Why am I here? Why does my life matter? What's the point of living?* If you fulfill God's purpose to love Him and love people, you can wake up every day with intention.

My mom would always tell my sister and me when she began to notice too many selfies on our Instagram pages. She'd say, "If you make your page about yourself, that's not going to turn out good either way. The negative comments can hurt you, and the positive comments can go to your head." She was right. The thing is, you'll be constantly trying to take a better selfie to one-up the last one. You'll end up in competition with yourself on what gets the most likes, and for what?

> YOU DON'T WANT TO SET YOUR LIFE UP TO LIVE IN YOUR OWN SHADOW.

Your social media profile is a picture of who you are. It's a page with your name, your bio, and posted pictures to show off what you're doing. It forces you to answer the question, *Who am I?* With every post, you can have some purpose behind it. But if you create a false version of who you are, then you're never going to feel fulfilled or that you're living out your purpose. Because really, you're hiding under a highly filtered mask. You don't want to set your life up to live in your own shadow. But if you use social media to represent who you actually are, and you use it for the better, it may help you find purpose.

Soon after Honey was born, I debated whether I wanted to post pictures of her. I had seen many celebrities hide their kids and so I thought that was probably the route to go. I ended up texting one of my good friends, Alexa PenaVega, who is a well-known actress, for advice because I had seen her sharing her kids on social media.

When I asked her what her thought process was about sharing their family's pictures online, she answered, "We asked ourselves, 'How do we best represent the kingdom on earth?' After all, we want to do that in every aspect of our lives. We want to shine a light on biblical values like family and set an example for faith-based families."

Wow, that is how you shine your light. That is how you bring purpose into your post.

It would have been easy for me to live in fear and hide Honey from the world. Sometimes, if I am honest, *I* want to hide from the world. But Jesus did not call us to be a lamp underneath a stand; He called us to be a city on a hill. Recently a young woman with her baby girl in her arms and tears in her eyes walked up to me and thanked me for helping her become a better mom through my example on social media. I am grateful for a friend who encouraged me to use my platform for a purpose.

Let's go back to the idea of God as our Creator. Creation around us does not miss a day to fulfill its purpose. "The heavens proclaim the glory of God. The skies display his craftsmanship. Day after day they continue to speak; night after night they make him known. They speak without a sound or a word; their voice is never heard. Yet their message has gone throughout the earth, and their words to all the world" (Psalm 19:1–4 NLT).

I love how this passage says although the skies cannot be heard, their message is heard throughout the world. You don't have to be the loudest one out there, but let your life live out your purpose. You will be surprised how many you reach and help to find what they are searching for.

Comparison, competition, and showmanship on social media are not the path to purpose and happiness. It's not sustaining to want glory for yourself, to seek the constant affirmations, and to savor the compliments. In fact, those things never leave you secure; they always leave you wanting more. You'll never reach an amount of likes or followers that will fulfill you.

> IF WHAT YOU HAVE NOW IS NOT ENOUGH, IT WILL NEVER BE ENOUGH. IF YOU ARE LOOKING IN THE WRONG PLACES TO FIND YOUR WORTH YOU WILL NEVER FIND IT.

When I was seventeen years old, shortly after I was on *Dancing with the Stars*, I went to a conference and heard a pastor speak some words that hit me hard. He said, "If what you're filling your life with right now is not enough for you, it will never be enough." In that moment it felt like every other person in the room disappeared for a minute and he was speaking directly to me. I realized that I had been looking for fulfillment and purpose in the wrong places. I had been so stressed about where I should go or what I should do next in life. Well, my next move was actually really simple: I walked up to the altar at that conference and got baptized. I realized that Jesus was the only One who is enough. He is the only One worthy of my praise and pursuit.

Friends, if what you have now is not enough, it will never be enough, because if you are looking in the wrong places to find your worth you will never find it.

The Only Way to Satisfy the Soul

I've experienced fame, but I haven't gained my value, purpose, or worth from that fame. I haven't found my joy or contentment from the followers who have liked my pictures. I can tell you that truthfully because, as you have seen, it was in some of my more famous moments that I struggled the most. The fame in and of itself wasn't the problem; placing my confidence in it was the problem.

I realized that people often try to get from their fans and followers what they can only get from whom *they* follow—if they're following the One whose love never ends. I am talking about Jesus and only Jesus. No amount of fame, money, or success can satisfy what the soul craves; we will only get what our soul craves by following Jesus Christ.

It's tough to remember that, though, when we get caught up in how people are (or are not) responding to us. We have to remind ourselves of how Jesus relates to us. Here are some truths you can come back to repeatedly so you can remember the one who defines you:

- I don't have to have followers to know I'm wanted. I know I'm wanted because the One I am following bought me with a price. (1 Corinthians 6:20)
- I don't have to have followers to know that I am liked. I know I am loved because the One I am following loved me enough to die for me. (John 3:16)
- I don't have to have followers to know someone cares about me. I know I am cared for because the One I am following knows every hair on my head. (Luke 12:7)
- I don't have to have followers to be socially accepted. I know I am accepted because the One I am following forgave me at the cross. (Ephesians 1:7)

ASK YOURSELF:

What are some specific situations in which you can imagine yourself when you'll want to remind yourself that you are wanted, loved, and cared for by Jesus?

Followers Follow a Purpose, Not a Person

When I started preaching, I had a hard time speaking to big crowds. My nerves would take over when I thought about all the people who would be watching me. I had a lot of anxiety and always felt a little uncomfortable and uneasy. The first time I was asked to speak somewhere was because of our family show *Duck Dynasty*. I got up for what was supposed to be twenty minutes and talked for only five minutes. People literally asked for their money back. Yikes. Rough start, huh? I'd like to say it got better after that, but first it got worse.

When I moved to Nashville at nineteen years old, I still had this dream in my heart of what I wanted to do. I was struck by a calling to speak and connect with others to share the Word of God. It was a big, intimidating calling, and I had no idea where to begin.

I was told by a few people in the speaking business that to be successful, I would have to sign with a big agency. I was able to meet and sign with a well-known record label who represented many musicians and artists. I thought it was so cool and amazing they believed in me, and with their support, I would get to do what I wanted to do. They made trumpeting promises, like I would have a tour every year, and they would support me in multiple ways. I thought that this was how I would best be able to influence and encourage my generation.

Unfortunately, it was a horrible partnership. They ended up unintentionally steering me away from who I felt I had been called to be and what I wanted to do. But I realized that I didn't need to follow the established way of planning speaking engagements to share the Lord's message and connect with others. I could just keep doing what I was already doing, continuing in the ways God had already been using me.

If God has put something in your heart to do, then He will open the doors to do it. That one tour I did with the agency was kind of a flop. We even had to cancel two shows because we had sold only forty-five tickets in the whole arena. Talk about humble beginnings!

I eventually left that partnership and created my own grass-roots tour. The corporate tour had been about putting on a performance, but that's not what I'm about. I stripped all the performance aspect away and got back to basics. My goal was, and still is, to simply talk like a human, to relate with others about our triumphs and struggles, and to share the power of the Word.

The turnout was incredible. In fact, the tour sold out. I felt so connected with everyone we met. I think it was the purity of my words and message—the raw, organic beauty of relating to people—that shifted the energy.

It can be tempting to follow someone who seems to have it figured out, especially when you don't know who you are. But it's essential to get clear on where they're leading you. More often than not, they just talk a good talk and then you get stuck. Lots of people stay in those situations for too long instead of leaving and trusting that God has something better for them.

It also can be tempting to take the option that gives you the quickest path to success. The offer I took was so enticing because it made many things I wanted to do instantly available. Social media and apps give us such a quick fix and feeling of gratification, but sometimes the route that God wants you to take will not be the quickest one, and that's a good thing. He wants to grow you on the journey. I am glad my tour didn't sell out right away;

I can see now that God made it happen at the perfect time, when I actually had something worth saying.

How you're leading also indicates how people are following you. That performance-style tour was setting me up to be a celebrity, to be famous. The other way—my way—was setting me up to be a good friend, somebody real.

I once heard Pastor Mike Todd say something that has stuck with me: "All you have is all you need."[12] I felt so humbled that God would use me in this position. I always understood that the glory and credit went to Him, because I knew His strength was made perfect in my weakness (2 Corinthians 12:9). I genuinely hid under the shadow of God's wing, and I still do as I go up on any stage. I was putting myself in front of people for Him, not for me, and that is what kept me going. I'm doing this to influence people toward Jesus, not to get people to follow me. Once I realized this, I was able to fully step into my calling and into my faith with confidence. It is amazing how fear begins to go away the less you think about yourself. Fear left when I realized I did not have to be confident in myself or my ability. I can be confident in the Lord and what He is doing through me, and that's all I need.

Perspective Shift

There is a scripture that has been so transformative in my life that I pretty much share it every chance I get—I've included it in every book I've written and said it in more sermons and conversations than I can count. It's Hebrews 10:35: "Do not forget the confident trust you have in the Lord, for which you will be richly rewarded" (my paraphrase).

When I began to understand that my confidence doesn't come from me, that it comes from my confident trust in the Lord, everything changed. Just a few years ago, I felt so insecure, afraid, and anxious. Once I made this perspective shift and realized the spotlight is not on me but on the Lord, it freed me to be me. When I was hyperaware of the fame, I struggled. But when I realized the focus was on Jesus, not on me, I stepped into the spotlight willingly and comfortably, and prayed that His light in me would shine even brighter than the spotlight.

Maybe you need to make that same shift to do the things you feel called to. Maybe once you think of yourself less you can actually start that project, call that person, invite those people over, and make the next move, realizing it is not about you but about a greater purpose. I often see people waiting to step into their purpose and experience the blessing of living in confidence because they are waiting on people to validate them. They instead could be gathering behind the King of kings and letting God Himself validate them because of how He made them.

When I started to become more recognizable to the public, I looked around to see who else had achieved something similar to what I wanted to do. I wanted a role model because I was looking to make a life change. It's always good to consider what others are doing in similar positions and see if you can learn from them. When I started looking at young women who got famous at a young age, I actually began to feel more scared, because not a single one looked like me or what I was going for.

People who interviewed me and wrote articles about me often compared me to singers and actresses who came from small towns or the South, or people who appeared on reality shows, or entertainers who came up at a young age, and I didn't like what they were insinuating. The underlying message was, *If Sadie thinks she's innocent and has faith now, let's see what the spotlight does to her.* It felt like a waiting game; the world was watching to see if I would lose it or not. And that really scared me. Because I didn't want to change like that. It caused me a lot of turmoil until I realized something critical. *I didn't have to change.*

Here's the thing: just because everyone else changes or does something does not mean you have to. Just because everyone else chooses to live a certain way does not mean you have to. You can be the role model for someone else.

To be honest, shortly after that first tour flopped, when I chose my path and started following Jesus in fame, I didn't think I would continue to have a big following. I thought once I went all in for Jesus my fifteen seconds of fame would pass, but that didn't bother me. It was the hill I was willing to die on, if you will. I knew it was not the popular route, but by doing what I did and standing for what I believed in, I found millions of people who were looking for that role model.

There are few times that you get to see and appreciate the effect of your influence, but knowing what's possible fuels me more than any number of followers or attention ever could. I recently interviewed two young women for our podcast whose story, more than any other, continues to inspire me and remind me of the power of authentic, positive influence.

In 2020 I spoke online for Passion City's Easter service, and right before I did, I shared about it on TikTok. One of the women saw my post and decided to watch. She had not been to church in years, but she figured it'd be a nice thing to watch on Easter. After watching, she gave her life to Jesus. Then she told her sister to watch the second service, and her sister watched, was similarly moved, and decided to give her life to Jesus too. Their brother also ended up giving his life to Jesus.

I would never have known about this except they reached out to the church I spoke at and told their story of how their family had been changed for the better. I have the unique joy of knowing that story, and that is where I derive my sense of accomplishment. Not from followers, media interviews, or boxes of "free" stuff from brands, but from testimonies.

I take what I post seriously because I believe that what you share can impact somebody's life. I not only believe that but have actually seen it several times. The cool thing is, *you* have this kind of influence too. Sure, you might not have millions of followers, but you never know how much impact your post might have on the two hundred—or even ten—people who follow you. Even the difference you make in one life is enough. You never know who that person could reach, and who the next person could reach, and on and on. Every single person has the potential to reach thousands, potentially millions, when you think of it like this.

And let's be real. Although we may be inspired by the lives of people we follow online, our own lives are typically changed by the ones who really walk with us. So don't count yourself out.

You have the potential to be an influence on so many people right in front of you.

When people post even just a Bible reference, I usually look it up and read it. Imagine how you could impact someone by simply doing that or by sharing a sermon or podcast you listened to. You never know what conversations could open the door with the people who follow you or the people who are actually in your life. You can spark curiosity in people's hearts, and you can either lead them to something good or something bad.

Don't forget that you're influencing people one way or another—making someone else feel insecure, or making them feel inspired and affirmed, and sending them off to succeed in whatever they're doing. Having an overall purpose for your posts will help you do this. Do I intentionally attach purpose to every single thing I post? No. Sometimes I just post silly dance videos or a picture of my dog, but I live my life on a mission to love God and love people and that should always come through on my platform. Why not be intentional about bringing something positive into people's lives? Why not pursue that as part of your purpose today?

I hosted Dr. Daniel Amen, one of America's leading psychiatrists and brain health experts, on my podcast and he said something profound that affirms the value of pursuing our purpose: "Purposeful people are happier. Pleasure is actually the enemy of happiness, because when you get too much pleasure it wears out your pleasure centers. That's why early fame is not good for your brain. It wears out your pleasure center so then you feel flat. Too many people want followers and fame, and I am not so sure that is a great thing."[13]

Pursuing something only for pleasure through fame, money, or success will dwindle away in time, but pursuing something with purpose will sustain you for a lifetime. Dr. Amen said it perfectly: "If you know why you are on the planet, you are going to be happier."[14] Whoa, that's good!

We each have a unique purpose, but we also unite in shared purposes with like-minded people. So I've got a question for you: Do you want to join me in making a culture shift? Culture is the way it is because of what we do, and the only way to change it is to do something different. Who knows? We just might find that a whole lot of people have been waiting on the "something different" to join.

Start where you are today, right now. Be the change you want to see in your job, in your friend circle, on social media, and in the world. I'll be doing it where I am too.

WHEN WE PURSUE PURPOSE INSTEAD OF FAME, WE'LL FIND WHAT IS MOST VALUABLE: LOVING GOD AND LOVING OUR NEIGHBOR.

what are you sharing and why?

In anonymous seasons we must hold tightly to the truth that no doubt strengthened Jesus throughout his hidden years: Father God is neither *care*-less nor *cause*-less with how he spends our lives. When he calls a soul simultaneously to greatness and obscurity, the fruit—if we wait for it—can change the world.

ALICIA BRITT CHOLE[1]

*SEVERAL YEARS AGO, I WAS IN A VERY PUBLIC RELATION-*ship, in a very public season of my life. The truth of what others saw on social media was not always the truth about this relationship. Many times we were so unhappy, and literally arguing, and one of us would post a cute couple picture showing we were

#couplegoals. Other people's affirmations made me feel comforted that even though we were unhappy, at least we looked happy. I know that's messed up, but I think a lot of us do this.

Publicly, it looked like we were a happy, supportive couple. But privately, I was spending a lot of time crying and feeling miserable. We were both unhealthy in this relationship, but we sure did look good on social media. The support for us on Instagram was strong, and I wanted the hashtags and the sweet comments to be true. Strangely, they almost convinced me that it was true. Every now and then we would have good moments that made me think, *Well, maybe things are going to turn around.* The relationship wasn't all bad, but it was bad enough that I knew it needed to end. I also knew that breaking up would be something I had to deal with publicly, and so for far too long we kept pretending our relationship was working, fooling the world on social media. But really we were fooling ourselves.

Many of us put so much time and energy into our outward appearances and not so much time and energy into how we're feeling, how we're connecting with others, God or our faith, our hopes and dreams, or our health and bodies. We just try to take a good angle and filter photos, write witty captions, and hope it shows that we're happy when maybe we're really not.

That will last you about as long as your makeup foundation. You work hard to make your foundation match your skin to cover up blemishes, and you coat your face to cover what is truly you. As the day goes on your foundation begins to wear off, crack a little, and all of a sudden what is underneath comes out. And what is underneath is what you are faced with every morning and every night. Instead of working to improve your skin, you work to cover it, but no matter how much you cover, you will always have to face your true self. It is the same with social media. You can filter and edit your caption to make it look perfect, but when you get off the app you will be faced with you.

Looking back, I now realize that I used to put way too much effort into my public life and not nearly enough into my private one. I spent way more time making sure I looked good and presented myself well than actually making sure that I *was* good and well. Honestly, half the time I really wasn't. It took awhile, but I finally figured out that although my private life might not sound as exciting as my public life, without a healthy private life I'll never have a sustaining public life.

ASK YOURSELF:

Are you putting more effort into your public life or your private life? If you want to invest more in your private life, what changes could you start making this week?

Privacy over Platform

Our generation is not as comfortable with creating and maintaining a private life as generations past. We're the voyeuristic, share-everything generation. A lot of times I think we don't even mean to get to the place we do when we publicly become something we aren't and need to maintain the image people see and like. Notice I did not say the image people "know and love"? Remember, those are two different things. But often we publicly become something that we aren't and then we have to keep it up. We end up having to live in that secret, hidden life instead of our purposeful, private one.

It took real intentionality for me to maintain a private life. A reset button, if you will. I had to learn how *not* to post everything about my life before I even had time to process it. Over the years—in my past books, on my podcast, and in sermons— I've talked about my struggles and the challenges I've faced. Everyone else probably knew more about who I was than I did. When I lived more publicly, I felt the extremes of every struggle intensify since they were shared with the world. I let the world's input on who they thought I was and who they thought I should be get into my heart.

Sweet Honey

The day that I went into labor with my baby girl was truthfully one of the greatest days of my life. While it was everything I had prayed for, it was nothing I had planned for. Let me expand on that a little bit.

I consistently prayed the whole time I was pregnant that she would have strong lungs. I prayed this because when I was pregnant with her, I got COVID-19.

It was a hard battle to fight. I had never felt that sick before, and I was also struggling mentally. Physically I was very weak and feeling depleted. I didn't even have the energy to read! And mentally I felt depressed from being so lonely while being sick. What helped me get through was worshiping even when I didn't feel like it and even when it was hard. Sometimes that included me singing with the music blasting and sometimes my worship looked like tears rolling down my face as I just listened to the words that I believed in my heart. A few lyrics in particular prompted me to keep praying that Honey would be born with such strong lungs that she'd be able to give a loud cry and make a sound of praise. I'd think of Psalm 8:2, which says, "Through the praise of children and infants you have established a stronghold against your enemies, to silence the foe and the avenger."

I had planned for an all-natural birth. In my mind I would be on a walk and out of the blue, my water would break. I would scream with joy, get Christian, grab the hospital bag, and rush to get there just in the nick of time to have our baby. You know, like you see in the movies. I wanted that story so badly.

Week after week passed and I tried *everything* on Google's list for how to induce labor—and nothing. I went in for my forty-one-week appointment, and my doctor expressed that the safest option would be to get induced. Again, not what I had planned, but for the safety of both the baby and me I decided to listen to his wisdom.

I went to the hospital that night for my doctor to induce labor. I labored through the night, and the next morning I had a magical moment—my water broke. Hours later I was pushing.

Up until this point it was honestly the most incredible experience. The anticipation to meet our daughter made even labor the most fun time. We had worship music going all day long and just felt close to heaven as we anticipated a miracle.

I had been pushing for about forty-five minutes, and then the doctor said that my next push would get her here. As I went in for the last push, things suddenly got chaotic; nurses pushed me down flat on my back, then pushed my stomach and pulled my legs as the doctor stood over me. A long two minutes and ten seconds later, my baby girl was out—but not breathing.

It turns out that Honey's shoulder had gotten stuck and was closing off her umbilical cord, keeping her from breathing. They got her out and rushed her to the table, expecting to have to rush her to the NICU for oxygen and to check her shoulder. All of a sudden the song "Million Little Miracles" came on, which could not have been more perfect for that moment.[2] And out of nowhere I heard it: Honey let out a cry. She'd started breathing.

The sound of life. The sound of praise. The sound of a miracle.

It truly was amazing, but I have to say it gave me a new point of view on what it's like to experience a miracle. A miracle typically comes from a place of need or desperation. Sometimes in the Bible that need would be rather unimportant, like a wedding that needed more wine, but other times that need would be desperate, like a woman who had been bleeding for twelve years and was an outcast in her community. Our desperation was for our baby girl to breathe so that she could experience life. The moments of desperation leading up to a miracle can be some of the most traumatic moments in life, whether they last twelve years or two minutes and ten seconds. And just because a miracle takes place doesn't always mean that everything is immediately back to normal.

After I had Honey, because of the intensity of those few minutes, I was in pretty rough shape physically. My stomach was bruised from the nurses having to push to get her out, and I had to be stitched for hours. The recovery was very hard. Why do I share all this with you? These are the things that no one knew and no one saw—even as they commented on my social media in the weeks that followed.

Here are actual comments I received:

"You must have not had a hard labor since you can stand up."

"She must not have required stitches because of the way she is out and about."

"Labor must have been a lot easier for her."

"She doesn't know what it's like to experience _____ in childbirth."

All of these were a result of me choosing to share the miracle of life with the public. I just chose to focus more on the miracle than on my suffering while I was taking time to heal physically, emotionally, and mentally in a private space with my family.

The Bible did something similar, didn't it? When we read the short story in the Gospels about the woman being healed from bleeding for twelve years, it focuses on the miracle of her healing. We don't read about her twelve-year journey of suffering with illness and enduring isolation. We don't read about how hard it was to return to a normal lifestyle after so many people knew her as having that condition.

When we read the story of Jesus healing a demon-possessed man, we hear about how he was healed. We don't hear about how traumatic it was for him when he wasn't in control of his body. We don't read about him living as a new man and Jesus follower in a place where everyone knew him as demon possessed. The amazing thing is that, because of our point of view as a reader, we always see Jesus.

In the Bible it is easy for us to see Jesus because we are looking for Him, but on social media it is a little harder. Maybe that is because when we look at social media we don't really look for Jesus. Often we instead look at what Jesus is doing in everyone else's life and not in our own.

I listened to a TED Talk by Michael Patrick Lynch titled, "How to See Past Your Own Perspective and Find Truth." It was an absolutely brilliant presentation about knowledge polarization. He touched on three points to help us see that we live in a common reality, which can help us have a healthier perspective of what we see online: we have to believe in truth, we need to be able to "dare to know," and we have to have a little humility. His last two points in particular I find very relevant for us.

In his point on "dare to know for yourself," Lynch mentioned how we cannot get caught in "bubble knowing," or believing that we are always right. Instead, we need to dare to understand, risking the possibility that we could be wrong about a situation.

He then noted how crucial it is that we approach what we see online with humility, defining this as "seeing your worldview as open to improvement by the evidence and the experience of others." The point is, you don't know it all. Arrogance is sometimes an easier approach than humility. It is easier to pride ourselves on what we think we know instead of giving an ear to understanding what we could be missing. He ended his presentation by saying, "Our perspectives, as wondrous, as beautiful as they are, are just that—perspectives on one reality."[3]

Life is all about perspective. Perspective is simply a point of view, and it is important to remember that just because we perceive something to be a certain way does not mean that we always get the full story and full picture. And most of the time the full story of someone else's life is not yours to know.

ASK YOURSELF:
When has someone had an inaccurate perspective of your life experience? When have you had an inaccurate perspective of someone else's? Based on what you've learned from these moments in your life, how do you want to respond to these kinds of differences of perspective in the future?

Vulnerability

Vulnerability is a big trend right now on social media, and there's a lot of pressure to share everything you're going through. I appreciate the move toward transparency and not sugarcoating our lives, and I acknowledge that it's difficult to share every struggle that you're going through. But I wonder if it's even worthwhile to share personal trials on a platform like social media. Vulnerability is an amazing gift to people who have empathy, who know your heart, and who you can trust. But vulnerability can be dangerous in the hands of those who don't know your heart or care to protect it. Brené Brown has said, "Shame cannot survive being spoken. It cannot survive empathy."[4] On the flip side, sharing our story with those who lack empathy can be the doorway to shame.

I once had an incredible conversation with Christine Caine on the podcast, and she gave some great advice. She told me, "Wait until your story becomes a testimony to share online."[5] Sharing all your problems all day may just amplify them, but waiting to see how Jesus moves and then sharing will give others hope. A lot of times, we just want to get a story out because it's relatable, and it's the thing that everybody's talking about. Instead, if you wait and let Jesus move, then you will be able to inspire people with how He can move in their own lives.

I think it is important to ask ourselves, Why are we sharing so many deeply personal thoughts online? At times vulnerability is being co-opted by those sharing for the sake of growing platforms or those seeking affirmation in the comments. But honestly, when done in a way that welcomes people in, vulnerability can inspire people to keep going. It could not only help a platform grow but also help a person grow.

When Christian and I started to date, I wanted it to be different from my past experiences. In fact, I did not even want to date him because I did not want to go into *another* public relationship like the ones I have mentioned, a relationship that ends and then is all over my Google search. I played it very casual at first and we took it very slow. When I knew that I wanted to date him, I let him know I did not want it to be public for a while because I did not want everyone else's opinions becoming part of our new relationship. He respected that and was on the same page. I wanted to guard his heart and my own.

So we dated privately. Not secretly, but privately. All our friends and family knew about us, and we spent so much time with those people. The ones who love us and speak wisdom into our lives witnessed us dating and shared in our joy. When we were confident in our relationship, we finally posted publicly. And guess what? It changed nothing because we were rooted.

If your roots are being watered by God's Word instead of the world's comments, it creates a true stability in your life. Jeremiah 17:8 says, "He is like a tree planted by water, that sends out its roots by the stream, and does not fear when heat comes, for its leaves remain green, and is not anxious in the year of drought, for it does not cease to bear fruit" (ESV).

Christian and I have a favorite passage from Psalm 1: "Whose delight is in the law of the LORD, and who meditates on his law day and night. That person is like a tree planted by streams of water, which yields its fruit in season and whose leaf does not wither—whatever they do prospers" (vv. 2–3). We love it because it inspires our relationship. We strive to be so planted and rooted in the Word of God with leaves that do not fade and fruit that does not die off; we believe that when we root ourselves in Him, nothing can tear us apart.

To us, this visual of a tree planted by a stream of living water shows us the necessity of living by the Word of God, remaining steadfast in our faith, and seeking life from the Lord and no other sources. When you're rooted strongly in the ground, adversity and hardships cannot topple you. You're able to deal with whatever comes your way. On the other hand, if you're a small flower or weed living on the daily watering of social media comments, views, likes, and retweets, your shallow roots can easily be pushed and pulled with the wind.

If you want to become like that strong, vibrant tree, then build your connection with the Lord every day. Think of how roots start unseen, in a hidden space, and once they're healthy enough, they can create something beautiful for people to see.

> IF YOUR ROOTS ARE BEING WATERED BY GOD'S WORD INSTEAD OF THE WORLD'S COMMENTS, IT CREATES A TRUE STABILITY IN YOUR LIFE.

I'm asked all the time, "How do you do what you do? How do you grow your platform and your audience?" I understand the question; so much value is placed on cultivating a large following as so many opportunities stem from it. But I don't see getting those opportunities as the goal, ever. I always respond by saying, "Let's not focus on growing your audience. Let's focus on growing yourself. Grow yourself into being someone worth following."

You can grow the largest following on social media, but just because it's huge doesn't mean it's a positive, healthy community. If you're posting content that compromises your values or stimulates the kind of controversy and provocation that gets attention, then you've got to ask, does the size of your following even matter? Those kinds of followers will come and go as the next interesting, trendy person comes along.

The way we move toward success matters. We see this in the book of Daniel, when King Nebuchadnezzar had a dream that carried a message from God. He dreamt of a big, strong, beautiful tree that reached high into the sky, providing shelter for animals and food for everyone. Then a holy messenger in the dream told him to cut the tree down all the way to the stump without uprooting it.

When Daniel interpreted the king's dream for him, Daniel said the tree represented the king and that "the command to leave the stump of the tree with its roots means that your kingdom will be restored to you when you acknowledge that Heaven rules." Then Daniel continued, "Accept my advice: Renounce your sins by doing what is right. . . . It may be that then your prosperity will continue" (Daniel 4:26–27).

The Lord told King Nebuchadnezzar that he needed to rebuild, knowing that all the power and success in his life wasn't ultimately about him; it was about the one and only true God. It wasn't actually his own earthly rule; it was all heaven's rule reaching down to earth. God wanted the king's heart to change and to "acknowledge that the Most High is sovereign over all kingdoms on earth and gives them to anyone he wishes" (v. 25).

If you've grown a social media following, become successful in your work or school, or accomplished something great, you could appear really strong and have a lot of followers and success. But if your route to that success hasn't been healthy, you might need to cut down to the stump and start regrowing. Why? Because it is not sustainable. I'm not talking about your business or your followers; I'm talking about your heart and making sure that it's growing in a way that is bigger than yourself.

The Value of Time

I took on this experience myself a few years ago when I went on a social media break for three months. It became a real turning point in my life when I started to connect with my calling as I got older and began to mature.

Before my social media break, I had always been a Christian. But I had never read my Bible as much as I had wanted to due to "lack of time." During those months without the distraction and influence of social media, I had the time and space to sit with God's words for the first time in my life. Every day I picked up my Bible and books instead of my phone. I immersed myself in His Word instead of in the trending stories and latest posts. I started taking my faith really seriously, and I became inspired.

There's a particular statement of Jesus' that convicted me (and still convicts me today): "It is out of the abundance of the heart that the mouth speaks" (Luke 6:45 NRSV). This verse guided me to protect what I put into my heart, especially because I had to speak publicly often! During that time without social media I had the chance to speak to my fellow college-aged Christians at the Passion City College Night, and I shared a message about pressing past any fear to fulfill the purpose God has for your life. This was my first time to preach a full message at a church.

That video went viral, with over one million views on YouTube and millions more on Facebook in multiple languages, and the positive reception is what led me to everything I'm doing now—even being on the Passion conference team with my husband! All of it happened after I took time to work on my heart and become knowledgeable about Scripture during a private season.

I was motivated to read more about God before I started telling people about Him. I wanted to understand more about my relationship with Him and what I truly believed, not just what people told me. In time, I did understand more. It helped that I didn't have to force anything publicly. I took the time to privately plant my roots in Scripture before sharing any messages publicly. And then eventually, sharing publicly just came naturally. I think people are bound to crumble when they try to force themselves to be something publicly that they really aren't privately.

Whatever you're putting in will come out. It's in those private times that we have to study, read, think, prepare, and cultivate. If I didn't study the Word, how would I preach? If your doctor did not study in school, how would she perform your surgery?

My social media break was inspired by a book called *Anonymous* by Alicia Britt Chole, which a friend gave me to read. The book mentions what Dick Schroder noted about God speaking the famous words, "This is my Son, whom I love; with him I am well pleased" (Matthew 3:17). Schroder noted that God spoke these words "*before* Jesus had ever *done* anything for which we call him Savior." The book goes on to say, "God sounded his affirmation from above over Jesus' life *before* Jesus ever preached one sermon or enlightened one mind, *before* Jesus ever healed one body or saved one soul."[6]

I was only nineteen when I read this book, but I had already lived much of my life publicly. During the years I was trying to figure out who I was and what I wanted to do in life, I had a lot of other voices telling me who I was and what I should do. I felt a lot of pressure from people, but I also put that pressure on myself when it came to my relationship with God. I thought I needed to do more or be better for Him to be proud of me or for Him to continue to use me.

Before I read *Anonymous* everything I did and everything I thought about immediately became a social media post. When I read a scripture, before I even got to the next one, I would stop and share it on my Instagram Story. When I heard a good quote in a sermon, I would stop the sermon to share it to my following. I was quick to share, which was not necessarily a bad thing, but as I shared these amazing messages before meditating on them myself, I was not getting the message into my own heart before I gave it to others. I was like a water balloon with a hole, constantly filling up but somehow always ending up empty. I needed to patch the hole for a minute and establish a solid relationship with Jesus myself before I tried to help others establish one as well. I wanted to make God proud by sharing things that helped other people, but He first wanted a relationship with me.

We see this aspect of God's character in Jesus' relationship with Peter. When their relationship was unsteady and it was time for them to reconcile and rebuild their connection, Jesus did not just go up to Peter and say, "You can fix our relationship by going and doing." He reestablished the love in their relationship before He told Peter to do a thing. He asked, "Do you love me?" before He said, "Feed my sheep" (John 21:17).

Jesus wants a relationship with us first before we go and do. The Father's affirmation from above comes *before* we ever do anything worthy of applause, attention, or love. The reason we struggle is that we crave validation from the world in the form of blue checkmarks, likes, or views, or through the right friend group or the coolest relationship—and we don't let God's affirmation send us out with confidence in who we are. Looking to the world's applause and attention to confirm that we are "good enough" keeps us from reaching our full potential. We're waiting on people who struggle with their own insecurity, jealousy, and self-worth to affirm us in our lives instead of letting the words of our Creator be enough.

> THE FATHER'S AFFIRMATION FROM ABOVE COMES BEFORE WE EVER DO ANYTHING WORTHY OF APPLAUSE, ATTENTION, OR LOVE.

ASK YOURSELF:

How are you trying to gain affirmation from others or from God? Do you believe that He accepts and affirms you today, *right now*, without you having done something to earn it?

Jesus had years of private life before He had a public life, and those private years made Him who He was in public. He knew who He was, what His mission was, and who His Father was, which enabled Him to press past the mockers, accusers, and flat-out haters. Thank God, literally, that Jesus understood the value of private time. But it is important to note that even after He lived such a public life, He always made sure to maintain an element of privacy. After many miracles, we read of Him going to the mountainside alone to pray.

While we don't know exactly what Jesus' private life looked like, we can get clues from the way He acted in public. We know that as a Jew He would have heard rabbis reading Scripture. He would have also participated in the traditional feasts and festivals and known the stories of the people in the Old Testament. The point is, Jesus wouldn't have known the scripture He quoted if He hadn't studied it in His private life. He wouldn't have been able to perform the miracles He did if He had not spent time with His Father, knowing what He could do.

I believe those prayers in that private space gave Him the ability to perform miracles in public places. This is a great example for us to mimic—whether that's deleting social media for a time to read the Word more, turning off the TV, or staying in for the night to study, practice, pray, or worship. Maybe it means being content for a little while with where you are and not letting the opinions and expectations of others push you to do what you're not ready to do.

People see me speak at big events like the Passion Conference and Live Original, but they don't see me up late at night studying the Word. And I don't need for people to see me doing that. For months before I ever got on stage, I prayed for God to give me the words that would impact a generation. Those types of moments I have with the Lord in private directly affect the moments when I am leading people in public.

> IF WE WANT TO IMITATE JESUS' LIFE, WE NEED TO SPEND TIME WITH THE FATHER PRIVATELY AND GIVE HIM GLORY PUBLICLY.

If we want to be like Jesus, we can't just look at His public life. We have to look at what He did in private. Ephesians 5:1 says, "Be imitators of God, as beloved children" (ESV). If we want to imitate Jesus' life, we need to spend time with the Father privately and give Him glory publicly.

Finally Rooted

You know what feels crazy to say? More than ever before, I know who I am. In fact, someone asked me recently who I was, and as

I thought about how to answer I realized that for the first time in a while, I actually do know who I am. This might be the first time in my life that I feel truly secure in who I am and what I do. It feels really good to be in this place, especially because it wasn't always this way.

When I married Christian, we created a normal, quiet life filled with our families and close friends. I noticed that in the normalization of my life and knowing who I am, I've never had more peace. I don't struggle with fear like I used to. I'm not insecure like I used to be. I feel confident in where I am. I don't feel the need to strive. I feel really content with what I do.

I think part of this comes from not trying to convince myself or anyone else that I'm someone I'm not. It comes from prioritizing my private life with God and rooting myself in His Word. I am finally able to be myself, not competing against a made-up image of someone I created.

Maybe you know exactly what I'm talking about because you're in that place too. Or maybe you think this sounds like a nice little daydream that's totally out of reach. Believe me, it is within reach! It was once just a daydream for me too. If you want to bring about a change in your life, start investing more in your relationship with God. Take out the things in your life that are stealing from the things that truly matter. Make your time with God the priority of your life. Then let Him lead you from there. Invite His love to strengthen you and His Word to give you confidence and peace.

IF YOU LET GOD'S WORD KEEP
YOU ROOTED AND GROUNDED,
YOU'LL BE MORE FOCUSED ON
GROWING HIS KINGDOM THAN
ON GROWING YOUR PLATFORM.

are you following cancel culture?

There's a big difference between liking Jesus and being like Him, and He said we would never be able to be like Him unless we loved our enemies.

BOB GOFF[1]

HAVE YOU EVER HAD AN AWKWARD FIRST DATE? THERE is just so much to navigate. You're trying to have genuinely good conversations by asking good questions, but you're also trying not to share too much. You're trying to act casual while also trying to look cute. First dates can definitely be exciting as you think about the potential relationship to come, but they're usually pretty nerve-racking and awkward. I actually thought Christian had a stuttering problem during our first several dates, which I thought was cute, but later I found out he was actually just super nervous!

When my family began filming *Duck Dynasty*, one of the executive producers told us, "Think of it like a first date. Don't talk about politics or religion. You have to get to know each other a little better first." Don't ruffle any feathers during the first impression stage—I get it. It makes sense to let the audience, or your date, get to know you a bit before you talk about the deeper things in life, the things on which you have potential to seriously disagree.

In today's culture, however, it's almost like we can never get to the point where we may express our views on important issues without the risk of saying the wrong thing and ultimately being canceled. Most people I talk to actually want to talk about the hard things, but they have this massive fear of the consequences in what is deemed as today's "cancel culture," so they just stay quiet.

> IF WE ARE TOO SCARED OF MAKING A MISTAKE TO TALK, TO ASK QUESTIONS, EVEN TO BE WRONG EVERY ONCE IN A WHILE, HOW WILL WE EVER GROW?

I don't think we are doing anyone any favors by not allowing for different thoughts, beliefs, and ideas. It's through this diversity of thought that we learn from one another, find better ways to do things, and ultimately grow. A few years ago, everyone was talking about tolerance. It feels like now tolerance is only a thing if you are agreeing with what the world tells you is popular and deemed acceptable to think—and that is constantly changing. It's hard to keep up! The thing is, if we are too scared of making a mistake to talk, to ask questions, even to be wrong every once in a while, how will we ever grow? When I think about cancel culture, I think of a growing tree getting yanked out of the ground, its roots dangling, no longer touching the soil. All growth stops at that moment.

Unfollow

This generation is faced with obstacles stemming from social media that other generations never had to go through or even imagine. One of these is the ability to unfollow someone. For a few generations they've had the ability to turn off the TV or the radio when they didn't want to hear what was being said, but the person on the TV would never have to know that someone turned them off. Today we have the power to click a button that says Unfollow or Mute, and we opt out of seeing that person's life and opinions.

It's not necessarily a bad thing to unfollow someone, and there are certainly times when it's a positive thing for you to remove something distracting or misaligned from your life. But we can't deny that the trend of unfollowing is affecting how we communicate and interact with people in the real world. Sometimes we unfollow people just because we don't know why we followed them in the first place. Other times we unfollow people to make a point—either to hurt them or let them know they hurt us in some way, or because we found out they did something egregious in the past that makes them unworthy to follow. These are the times I think unfollowing can be problematic.

The unfollow mindset enables us to see only the things and people that we agree with. In the past there was no getting around those you disagreed with: people lived in big families, many times multigenerational. People often worked in the same office and the same church for most of their lives. I believe the unfollow culture has impacted how we interact with the world. If we don't like our family's views, we simply move away from them. Many of us work from home so we don't have to interact with coworkers we differ with or don't like, whether it's their religion, politics, or personality. We jump from church to church in search of one that aligns perfectly with our wants and needs. I think that many in this generation struggle with commitment problems because of how easily they can unfollow others or be unfollowed themselves.

Many people see how many followers I have and think it must be great. It is great, but it's also humbling, because having a lot of follows means having a lot of unfollows. In any given week about five thousand new people will decide to follow me. Great, right? But in that same week about three thousand will decide to unfollow me. So yes, I did gain, but I also lost. Those numbers are real people who decided that they no longer want to see my stuff—and that is okay, because I unfollow people, too, but it can certainly make me question myself. The fear of losing follows because of the Unfollow button can keep people from putting themselves out there in the first place.

Here's how I look at it: everyone gets to follow whoever they want and that fact shouldn't be a big deal. It becomes a big deal when we bring the follow/unfollow mindset into our relationship with Jesus or with others. Yes, in life we can follow what we like and unfollow what we don't, and that is fair. But if we get too comfortable with following and unfollowing things that make us happy or comfortable, we lose both the ability to create true relationship and the importance of the word *follow*.

Your relationship with Jesus needs to be a commitment, not a convenience. To follow Jesus means the Unfollow button is nowhere in sight. It is not in sight when you don't like the way your day played out or when you don't like a scripture you read. You choose to follow Jesus no matter what the world throws at you and no matter how uncomfortable or unpopular it gets. Many people want to follow Jesus privately but unfollow Him publicly; they know following Him will save their lives but also cost them their reputations.

We've lost our ability, and sometimes even our desire, to commit. At the slightest provocation, we bail. We do that on social media, with celebrities, with friends, and even more so in our relationship with God—which is alarming because every relationship *will*

> YOUR RELATIONSHIP WITH JESUS NEEDS TO BE A COMMITMENT, NOT A CONVENIENCE.

get tough at some point. And when it gets tough, are we just going to walk away or unfollow because we did not like something?

I have seen people in real life not go to family holidays anymore because they have different political views than their loved ones. I have seen people refuse to speak to an old friend who posted something on social media they disagreed with. This mindset is making us isolate ourselves to the point that we no longer have real relationships with people. We only have people around us or online who agree with us. Your world can get really small if you surround yourself only with people who think, act, and talk like you. How could we ever learn or grow by listening only to things we already know?

Jesus set an example of sitting at the table with people who were not like Him, who lived very different lifestyles. Even His disciples were diverse in their workspaces and lifestyles before they met Him. He got into conversations with a Samaritan woman when it was not culturally acceptable for a Jew to talk to a Samaritan. He did life with Mary Magdalene, who was once demon possessed. He befriended many tax collectors. He ate with sinners. When Jesus opened Himself up to people who were different from Him, He gave others the opportunity to form a relationship with Him and ultimately be led to eternal life. If you open up your life to people who think differently than you, you might get to lead them to the cross.

Jesus didn't point us toward cancel culture. He didn't lead us toward turning our backs on each other and quitting when things get hard. He set us on a much different path, one that is so much more rewarding, even if it is more difficult.

Canceling people really is about ease, isn't it? The simple reality is, we just want to take the stress-free route. It's easy to unfollow someone. It's easy to call someone to task for misdeeds or a differing viewpoint. It's easy to take out your frustration on someone who's not standing right in front of you.

The negative comments on social media can be brutal. We can call people out and publicly ridicule them on social media until it basically feels like their life is over. When an unpopular or potentially offensive opinion, or an incorrect statement, is called out, the perpetrator is often personally punished and ostracized, losing followers, business relationships, and public and even private support. Cancel culture is a modern take on a centuries-old punishment of public shaming. Modes of public shaming have changed over time—from stocks in medieval Europe, to tarring and feathering, and even head shaving for political traitors.[2]

In the secular world today, punishment comes swift and hard. If someone says something politically incorrect, hateful, inappropriate, or easily misinterpreted, they are publicly called out, corrected, and maybe overcorrected. Being called out isn't necessarily a bad thing. We all screw up and say or do the wrong thing. When that happens, yes, it needs to be addressed.

Now I'm not saying that we shouldn't be accountable for the mistakes that we make or the things we say ignorantly that offend people. But holding someone accountable and canceling someone are two different things. We are not meant to harshly judge each other; we are supposed to make each other better. Can you imagine how much better our world would be if we took the time to help each other become better after making mistakes, instead of just casting each other out?

As this phenomenon has grown more pervasive, there is a sense that people are looking for mistakes and opportunities to tear down others instead of giving them the chance to learn and revise. The speed and readiness with which the masses call people out and seem to revel in punishing them is pretty scary. The resulting culture is negative and full of people being defensive and guarded.

ASK YOURSELF:
How do you find yourself joining in on cancel culture?
Who have you known who has been hurt by it?

A Dream, a Coat, and Cancel Culture

There is a story in the Old Testament about Joseph, one of the twelve sons of Jacob. Remember the story of the guy who married two sisters? We are talking about that Jacob. Joseph was Rachel and Jacob's son, and not only did Jacob love Joseph's mama, but he loved Joseph. He loved Joseph so much that he gave Joseph a coat of many colors and made it clear that he wanted him to have a lot of leadership and inheritance in the future. You might joke about being the favorite in your family, but in this family there was no doubt. Joseph was definitely the favorite.

It also did not help that Joseph had a gifting on his life. He was a dreamer. God gave him dreams and the ability to interpret them. One day Joseph decided to share some of his dreams with his brothers, including the ones with imagery showing that he would one day rule over all of them.

Israel [Jacob] loved Joseph more than any of his other sons, because he had been born to him in his old age; and he made an ornate robe for him. When his brothers saw that their father loved him more than any of them, they hated him and could not speak a kind word to him.

Joseph had a dream, and when he told it to his brothers, they hated him all the more. He said to them, "Listen to this dream I had: We were binding sheaves of grain out in the field when suddenly my sheaf rose and stood upright, while your sheaves gathered around mine and bowed down to it."

His brothers said to him, "Do you intend to reign over us? Will you actually rule us?" And they hated him all the more because of his dream and what he had said. (Genesis 37:3–8)

Here's some advice. If you have a dream like this as a teenager, it's probably an okay idea to tell your parents, but as far as your siblings, learn from Joseph's mistake and keep it to yourself! Because of his misstep, Joseph got the Old Testament version of cancellation.

Joseph spoke too soon about his dreams. He might not have been malicious or intended to hurt or belittle his brothers, but to tell them that he dreamed he would one day rule over them was a tough message for them to hear, especially since he was clearly already his father's favorite son. The anger the brothers felt toward him led them to do some horrible things.

> They saw him from afar, and before he came near to them they conspired against him to kill him. They said to one another, *"Here comes this dreamer. Come now, let us kill him and throw him into one of the pits.* Then we will say that a fierce animal has devoured him, and we will see what will become of his dreams." But when Reuben heard it, he rescued him out of their hands, saying, "Let us not take his life." And Reuben said to them, "Shed no blood; throw him into this pit here in the wilderness, but do not lay a hand on him"— that he might rescue him out of their hand to restore him to his father. So when Joseph came to his brothers, they stripped him of his robe, the robe of many colors that he wore. And they took him and threw him into a pit. The pit was empty; there was no water in it. (Genesis 37:18–24 ESV, emphasis added)

Joseph's brothers wanted to destroy him. They mocked his dreams and tried to take away that gift on his life saying, "Let's see what becomes of those dreams." They stripped Joseph of his robe and reframed the story of his life, telling their father that he had been eaten by an animal. They left him in an empty pit with no food or water. They canceled his gift, his purpose, his identity, his relationships, and his future.

It is important to note, however, that Joseph did not die that day. He was sold into slavery. And his story doesn't end there either. After getting falsely accused in Potiphar's house, where he was enslaved, he was thrown into Pharaoh's prison. While in prison he continued to have dreams and even interpreted dreams for other prisoners.

Fast-forward a few years of being in prison, and one of the men who had been in prison with him had been released and was again serving Pharaoh as a chief cupbearer. Pharaoh had a very strange dream and was desperate for someone to interpret it. They were calling in magicians and wise people trying to find someone who could help figure out these crazy dreams. The cupbearer remembered Joseph from prison and told Pharaoh that he knew someone who could interpret his dream.

> Pharaoh sent and called Joseph, and *they quickly brought him out of the pit.* And when he had shaved himself and changed his clothes, he came in before Pharaoh. And Pharaoh said to Joseph, "I have had a dream, and there is no one who can interpret it. I have heard it said of you that when you hear a dream you can interpret it." Joseph answered Pharaoh, "It is not in me; God will give Pharaoh a favorable answer." (Genesis 41:14–16 ESV, emphasis added)

I want you to notice something. Years and years after getting thrown into a pit, mocked, stripped, and sold for being a dreamer, Joseph was taken out of a pit for being a dreamer. The very thing everyone canceled him for when he had a moment of immaturity and spoke without much wisdom is the very thing that got him out of the pit and into the palace. He ended up being placed as second in command over all Egypt, and he saved many lives, including his family's, because of his ability to interpret dreams.

Now, I am not offering you a cheesy Christian quote that "your biggest mistake is your biggest blessing." What I am saying is that if you *don't* let the mistakes you have made and the negative things people have said about you shame you to the point of quitting, then God can still use you. Joseph did not quit when he was canceled. He did not quit when he was betrayed by his brothers or when he was mocked and his reputation was destroyed. He did not quit when he was in prison and it looked like there was no future for him. He kept going and he kept doing what God called him to do.

People cannot cancel your life. They can try to hurt you and they *can* hurt you, but if you don't stop, they cannot stop what God has set in motion.

ASK YOURSELF:

How has negativity from others pushed you toward quitting, and how have you responded? What would it look like for you to be like Joseph, who kept going and kept doing what God called him to do?

Jesus and Cancel Culture

I don't think a lot of people realize that Jesus was widely misunderstood and highly criticized during His life. You might not expect the Son of God to feel such turmoil and struggle, but He did—just like we all have, and then some. Throughout the Gospels people were constantly trying to cancel Him because He would do and say things the religious leaders deemed politically and religiously incorrect. In fact, Jesus is the most canceled person in the Bible and in history.

People in positions of power and popularity in Jesus' time were held to high levels of scrutiny, just as they are today. Society closely watched their every move and carefully listened to their every word. Jesus was very popular with the people, but He also suffered the hostility of many in power. Scribes and priests fought to have Him arrested, stoned, and killed. Popularity can lead to envy, and those who are jealous of someone else's success can be quick to seize an opportunity to take another down.

When people today think about Jesus, they often think about the celebrated, exalted Jesus. Do we forget what He endured the last few years of His life? He spent much of His time dealing with people

> POPULARITY CAN LEAD TO ENVY, AND THOSE WHO ARE JEALOUS OF SOMEONE ELSE'S SUCCESS CAN BE QUICK TO SEIZE AN OPPORTUNITY TO TAKE ANOTHER DOWN.

trying to trap Him into saying the "wrong thing" or driving Him out of their city. His life culminated in a series of public trials, where people shouted "Crucify Him!" and chose to save a murderer instead of Him. And then came the absolute worst form of punishment—death on a cross.

Jesus faced crowds calling for His crucifixion, even though He was an innocent man. Pilate, the Roman governor who presided over Jesus' trial, wanted to let Him go, but the crowds demanded that He be crucified. Jesus was so misunderstood and so hated. The crowd grew angrier and louder as they demanded what they perceived as necessary justice. And it worked. Though He was about to be released by Pilate, the angry crowd coerced Pilate into crucifying Him.

As Luke 23:20–24 says, "Pilate addressed them once more, desiring to release Jesus, but they kept shouting, 'Crucify, crucify him!' A third time he said to them, 'Why? What evil has he done? I have found in him no guilt deserving death. I will therefore punish and release him.' But they were urgent, demanding with loud cries that he should be crucified. And their voices prevailed. So Pilate decided that their demand should be granted" (ESV).

Can you imagine the power of a mob who can accomplish such act? Cancel culture embraces a very similar mob mentality. There is little compassion or desire for deeper understanding of context and motivation. Instead, the judgment begins with one and builds and builds until it becomes a loud, singular voice making demands with no regard for nuance and humanity.

Cancel culture and peer pressure have similar effects.

Sometimes we just cancel people because everyone else did, and standing up for that canceled person would get us canceled too. You can see this take effect on Pilate as the crowd pressured him into crucifying Jesus. "From then on Pilate sought to release him, but the Jews cried out, 'If you release this man, you are not Caesar's friend. Everyone who makes himself a king opposes Caesar'" (John 19:12 ESV).

In His life, Jesus had both followers and friends. He had followers who would come listen to every sermon He preached, to witness the miracles He performed, and to watch Him heal the broken. But He also had twelve friends, His disciples, and those were the people He did life with.

It's important to know the difference between your followers and your friends. Jesus had followers, He had friends, and He had haters; He had to deal with all of them just like we do. He prioritized it all very well. He was always present for His followers and showed up for them. He was very intentional with His friends. And He didn't let the people who misunderstood Him stop Him from what He was doing.

In your group of followers, you will have those who cheer you on and encourage you, but you will also have naysayers and haters. I'm sure most of my followers want to

> HE WAS ALWAYS PRESENT FOR HIS FOLLOWERS AND INTENTIONAL WITH HIS FRIENDS. HE DIDN'T LET THE PEOPLE WHO MISUNDERSTOOD HIM STOP HIM FROM WHAT HE WAS DOING.

follow me with good intentions, but some of them are just looking to troll. The same was true for Jesus as He spoke to His followers and performed miracles on His travels. There were those constantly on the lookout to catch something He said that was worth punishment. Luke 11:54 tells it plainly: "They wanted to trap him into saying something they could use against him" (NLT). They did their best. Here's one example from Matthew 22:15–22:

> The Pharisees went out and laid plans to trap him in his words. They sent their disciples to him along with the Herodians. "Teacher," they said, "we know that you are a man of integrity and that you teach the way of God in accordance with the truth. You aren't swayed by others, because you pay no attention to who they are. Tell us then, what is your opinion? Is it right to pay the imperial tax to Caesar or not?"
>
> But Jesus, knowing their evil intent, said, "You hypocrites, why are you trying to trap me? Show me the coin used for paying the tax." They brought him a denarius, and he asked them, "Whose image is this? And whose inscription?"
>
> "Caesar's," they replied.
>
> Then he said to them, "So give back to Caesar what is Caesar's, and to God what is God's."
>
> When they heard this, they were amazed. So they left him and went away.

They didn't get what they wanted, so they left Him and went away. If only we could be as wise as Jesus—always speaking truth but also not giving in and giving the haters what they want!

Jesus was misunderstood in His life by others putting Him in the box of their expectations. Today, you might even be the one misunderstanding Him. With someone as famous as Jesus, there is so much noise around Him, so many stories and legends, beliefs, and assumptions. People have put His Word and His deeds into different contexts and given them different meanings to serve their purposes.

ASK YOURSELF:

Have you taken the time to get to know the heart of Jesus through His Word? You might know of Him, but do you actually know Him?

It is only when we learn from the source that we can make up our minds. So strip away what you've been told and what you've heard. Go to the source and get to know Him. Don't just see the façade of Jesus. He was fully God but also fully human and extremely relatable.

Many people get turned off to the idea of Jesus because they've heard that if you love Jesus, then maybe you don't love certain types of people. That's actually the opposite of what it means to love Jesus. In the Bible, the greatest commandment, besides love God with all your heart and mind, is to love your neighbor as yourself. Certainly, there have been many groups of people throughout history who have said that they're Christians and have acted in hateful ways under the false shield of working for Jesus—but that's not true to the Word of God. Jesus' whole message is about love and compassion. Jesus is so seen, but not always known.

The most canceled person in history is the One who canceled our sin, our past, and even death for all of us, giving us hope for our future! He was canceled to the point of death, and yet He is our hope in the midst of cancel culture, because of the pathway He opened by remaining faithful to God's will.

Don't Cancel; Have Compassion

The Bible, God, Jesus, and the Holy Spirit are completely opposite of cancel culture. The Bible is filled with stories like Joseph's—when it looked like it was over, God had a plan. If you look at the Bible's story as a whole, it's amazing that God didn't cancel us when we, as humanity, contentiously went against Him and sinned. Instead of canceling us He sent His Son to save us, redeem us, and give us hope for a future. And even when the world tried to cancel Jesus, He proved He can't be canceled. He busted past the ultimate mockery and death to make sure you knew that you were loved and that life beyond this world is possible.

Jesus cancels your sin, shame, guilt, condemnation, self-doubt, sickness, and pain. No matter what people try to say about you or do to you, you can find your identity and future in the blood of Jesus. Cancel culture is in direct opposition to the words and teachings of Jesus. In cancel culture, you make one mistake and you're called out and cast out. But not with Jesus. He was a proponent of redemption and forgiveness, not cancellation and exile.

"Repent therefore, and turn again, that your sins may be blotted out" (Acts 3:19 WEB). The Bible shows us many stories that demonstrate the power and beauty of forgiveness. Our God believes in repentance and redemption, so why should we cast someone out for a transgression? We all deserve the opportunity to learn, to grow, and to do better.

No human is the judge of our lives—God is. And for those who think God is harsh, go read some stuff on social media and see if humans aren't too. The difference is God's wrath comes out of love. Ours comes out of hate and spite.

Humans don't have the authority to judge each other's lives or cancel each other for their mistakes. Consider the words of James: "Do not speak evil against one another, brothers. The one who speaks against a brother or judges his brother, speaks evil against the law and judges the law. But if you judge the law, you are not a doer of the law but a judge. There is only one lawgiver and judge, he who is able to save and to destroy. But who are you to judge your neighbor?" (James 4:11–12 ESV).

Words Like Honey

Let's go back to the Joseph story. What if, instead of throwing him in a pit, mocking him, and selling him, his brothers simply said, "We know that you have these crazy dreams, but when you say stuff like 'I will rule over you,' it makes us feel angry and like you think you are better than us." I just wonder if that would have opened the door for Joseph to have a little understanding and mature more in his speech. Again, God still used him, and his life wasn't over, but he did have to go through so much pain, prison time, and a couple of pits to get there.

Cancel culture, criticism, and people going after each other breed so much negativity. I hope it's not the legacy of our generation. It's hard to reach your full potential when there's so much negativity coming at you or surrounding you. It can be difficult to stay positive and find the encouragement to push through. We need encouragers now more than ever.

There is a proverb that says, "The tongue has the power of life and death" (Proverbs 18:21). That's a huge statement, right? The words we say are going to either produce life in others or lead them toward death. *Words matter.*

Our daughter is named after another proverb: "Gracious words are a honeycomb, sweet to the soul and healing to the bones" (16:24). The irony of our daughter being named after this verse is that, when we announced her name, although we had a majority of kind and supportive comments, we had some terribly hateful ones too. People shared their opinion about how they didn't like her name in mean-spirited ways. As they were commenting I just kept thinking those people could use a little honey. We need more gracious words.

To thrive in such a negative environment, it's up to you to guard your heart, mind, and soul. And sometimes, if social media is bringing negativity into your life, remember the importance of intentionality around what you seek. Simply remove yourself from it for a minute to get healthy again.

Don't let those voices be louder than the ones in your life. Listen to your own family and friends, your own husband and pastor. Don't let people who don't know you be your source of truth; turn to your loved ones and the Bible. Let the people who truly know you speak life into you. We need the church to speak life abundantly.

The one positive aspect of cancel culture is that it forces us to think or pray a little longer before we put something out there. It's holding us to a higher standard. Joseph, for example, might have thought a little longer about sharing his dream with his brothers. "Everyone should be quick to listen, slow to speak and slow to become angry" (James 1:19).

There will probably still be people who set out to misunderstand you. No matter what you say or do they will just miss it—just like they missed Jesus. Remember you're not alone in that.

Same Destination

I was on a plane recently with my mom, and it occurred to me how different everyone on the plane probably was, yet we were all sitting peacefully, interacting cordially, and minding our own business. I wondered, if everyone's social media page popped up above their heads, what we would see. Would two people with opposing views get into an argument? Would one person body shame another? Would race, religion, geography, values, and the myriad other things that come between people start to play a role? If the plane became the social media environment, we might see the same kind of rudeness, intolerance, and impatience we do online. We might see the same attack mode of an angry mob, the one that normally hides behind their screens.

Just like when we are on a plane, in real life we are all going to the same destination. We're all going to die one day. Hopefully we're all trying to live a good life, even if we have disagreements on how that should look. But we've lost the mutual respect for how other people are in real life. There's too big of a disconnect between what people put out on social media and how they live their lives.

For example, there is a life rule that you are never supposed to ask a woman if she is pregnant. Well, before I was actually pregnant, I posted a picture of Christian and me attending a friend's rehearsal dinner. I personally loved my dress until I saw all the online comments asking if I was pregnant because they thought they saw a bump! Why do we act so different online than we do in person? You know not to ever say that to someone in person, but online, a place where we have thousands of filters, it ironically feels as though people have none. That doesn't mean you don't put out what you believe (unless that belief is that someone is pregnant—keep that to yourself), but do so respectfully, kindly. We need to have more integrity to interact on social media the way we live in person.

When you're faced with people who have different beliefs, values, judgments, and opinions, you can either choose to respect them and inspire them with your own beliefs, or you can get angry and fight. It's just like when you're little and your mom says to use your words instead of throwing a tantrum. You need to express yourself in a respectful way if you want the conversation to have any chance of making an impact.

My friend Elisabeth Hasselbeck used to be a cohost on the ABC daytime talk show *The View*. She was on a show with other women who had very different opinions on things than she did. She shared with me that, after spending so much of her time trying to prove she was right, she finally decided, "I do not want to be so right that I am wrong with people."

People are more important than the point you are trying to make.

My family has a show called *At Home with the Robertsons* on Facebook Watch. One of the concepts of the show is that we invite people to come to our house who think differently than we do or live a different lifestyle than we do. The goal is that we all learn from one another in the process. On one episode we hosted a vegan chef, and my dad is known for having a business that revolves around hunting. You can imagine we had some differences.

The coolest thing about the whole experience is that we genuinely love every guest we have on the show and we really do learn from them. People online seemed to have more of a problem with it than we did, and we were the ones sitting at the dinner table with people we did not agree with on certain topics. You would not believe the hateful things people said about my dad just because he ate a vegan meal to respect our guest. This is a great example of Elisabeth's quote. My dad did not want to act so right that he treated someone wrong. We have to remember that agreeing is not a requirement for love, but respect is.

When there's no respect, we don't feel safe enough to share our opinions. And if we're afraid of showing our true selves, how can we ever be seen and known? How can we use our voice and what we have to make the world better if we fear getting thrown into the modern-day pit? If we make a mistake, and we're torn down for our transgression by the angry online mob, how can we humble ourselves to learn and grow?

> IF WE CAN LEVEL OUR VOICES ENOUGH TO BE HEARD, WE CAN SHARE AND CONNECT IN PEACE.

If we can level our voices enough to be heard, we can share and connect in peace. We need to allow one another to continue to grow, to make mistakes and learn from them. We need to listen to others' perspectives with respect and love, check them against our own beliefs, and keep growing our roots deep. We need to forgive and offer grace, because it has been given to us by Jesus Christ.

GIVE PEOPLE SECOND CHANCES.
SEEK TO UNDERSTAND PEOPLE,
NOT JUDGE THEM. FOLLOW THE
TRUTH EVEN WHEN IT'S HARD.

does God still love you?

We cannot embrace God's forgiveness if we are so busy clinging to past wounds and nursing old grudges.
T. D. JAKES[1]

ARE YOU THAT DUCK GIRL?" THAT QUESTION USED TO realllly get to me. Sometimes I would simply reply yes, because I obviously knew what they meant, but I have to admit there were times I said no. I even would tell the pastors at churches where I was speaking not to say anything about Duck Commander or *Duck Dynasty* when they introduced me, not because I wasn't proud of it, but because it seemed like that was the only thing people knew about me. I was trying to start something new, like ministry, speaking, and writing, but it felt like I was just stuck being "that duck girl." I did not want to be known just for what I had done; I wanted to be known for who I was.

The struggle between who we were and who we are is a tension that many of us know well. It can be difficult to let go of our past and how we used to be known to others, whether it involves positive or negative experiences or a little bit of both. It can feel hard to be confident and worthy of stepping forward in a new way—especially in the age of social media, where it seems our past is never far behind.

We live in a time when everything is posted for everyone to see. Most posts are fun and filled with good memories, but some are meant to hurt or embarrass others. And some posts show people in situations they never should have been in. Mistakes, misjudgments, and moments of weakness and rebellion live forever online, preserving our lowest moments. I have had friends whose reputations were clouded because of posts from a not-so-good past—not only others' posts about them but their own posts when they were living a wilder life. Girls have told me how they weren't accepted into a sorority or they didn't land their dream job because of damaging posts, texts, or tweets from years past that have stayed with them.

It can be difficult to convince those around you that you've changed. I've talked to people who have turned their lives around only to struggle with others accepting their new life choices. It is tough when you get past the hardest part of forgiving yourself and then have to face the people who want to remind you of what you did. I've seen people gripped by fear that pictures they sent or words they posted online will come to the surface one day and they will be humiliated. That shame about who they used to be often keeps people from becoming who they are meant to be.

When we hang on to the past, we get stuck where we are instead of moving forward to where we're going. Whether we do it to ourselves or it's pushed on us by others, it's unfair that online records force some of our worst moments to relentlessly haunt us. But just because life happened and the pictures show something from our past doesn't mean we have to stay stuck. There is a way for us to let go of past mistakes and transgressions, and that way is with Jesus.

> SHAME ABOUT WHO THEY USED TO BE OFTEN KEEPS PEOPLE FROM BECOMING WHO THEY ARE MEANT TO BE.

Paul, a man who had a bad past himself, put so plainly why we can and need to move forward and not stay stuck where we are or where we were: "What shall we say then? Are we to continue in sin that grace may abound? By no means! How can we who died to sin still live in it? Do you not know that all of us who have been baptized into Christ Jesus were baptized into his death? We were buried therefore with him by baptism into death, in order that, just as Christ was raised from the dead by the glory of the Father, we too might walk in newness of life" (Romans 6:1–4 ESV).

> **ASK YOURSELF:**
> Are you walking in the newness of life, or are you stuck in the past? In what ways does your life now still look like the life you are wanting to leave behind?

The question then becomes, *How do I become who I am when everyone knows me for what I did or who I was?* I've heard this so many times, and I've even lived the story.

When Christian and I started dating, we talked about Jesus all the time. We shared podcasts with inspirational messages, Bible passages we were reading, the latest worship song we loved, and anything and everything Jesus was doing in our lives. That was naturally how our relationship formed because that was who we both were and what we both talked about.

Christian and I formed this relationship based on who we were at that time. This was the only version of Christian I knew because of who he was when we met and who he consistently was as we started dating. He and I didn't grow up in the same place; we did not meet until he was going into his junior year of college and I was living in Nashville. I didn't know Christian's past and he didn't know mine. I never knew who he used to be and he didn't know who I used to be before we each drew close to Jesus. And it turns out, Christian was pretty wild in high school and lived a very different life than the one he lived by the time I met him.

After he graduated high school, Christian went on to college, and his first semester was also pretty wild. Just your stereotypical college start. One night at a party, Christian was shotgunning beers on a balcony, and this guy walked up to him and said, "I thought you didn't drink!" The guy said this because Christian had joined his fraternity saying he was a dry pledge, even though he did drink—he just knew it was something he probably should not have been doing. But that night, on the balcony of his frat house, he looked at the guy and said, "You're right. I don't drink." In that moment he realized that what he was doing was not aligning with who he wanted to become.

Christian walked two miles home that night in the rain. He got back to his dorm, got on his knees, and prayed to God. After that, he turned his whole life around. He got involved with the church and started serving, and he made this amazing group of friends who shared and supported his values. They even started a Bible study on campus that very quickly grew to have more than one hundred guys! He totally changed. It's pretty incredible. Really, it's a miracle. It's one the Bible says will happen when you give your life to Jesus.

Even though Christian had become this new creation and was on fire for God when we met, I started to notice that some "past posts" were still making him feel the need to hide. When Christian would go home, he felt as though his family all knew him as his high-school self because that was the last version of him they'd seen. They didn't know the man he had become. He tended to revert back to the same attitude he had in high school when he was around people who knew that former version of him. He really struggled with going back to the place that held so much of the past that he was not proud of. He wanted to be who he was, but pressing past the past is hard. He wondered, *How do I press past who they knew me to be and show them who I actually am now?*

Now, I didn't know any of this during our first visit with his family—so that made for some weird moments. When I casually brought up Christian's relationship with Jesus in front of his family, I noticed he didn't want to talk about it. I thought it was super strange he was being so evasive and awkward, because with me he was always so open and confident about it.

The funny thing is, all his family members are believers who love Jesus and love Christian. But the enemy has a way of making you feel stuck. And as long as he can keep you stuck in who you used to be, he does not have to worry about the miracle you have become.

HOW DO I PRESS PAST WHO PEOPLE KNEW ME TO BE AND SHOW THEM WHO I ACTUALLY AM NOW?

I encouraged Christian to share his story with his family. Part of his hesitation, though, was that telling them how far he had come would expose the whole truth of who he was before. His family had never known just how wild he had been, and it would be hard for him to tell them. But he did it anyway. He finally told his parents all about how he used to live and what had changed for him when he got to college. He shared that he was on fire for the Lord.

Of course, his parents were so proud of him. They are such loving parents. The honest conversation created a freedom with his family to talk openly about what God was doing in his life and to be proud of where he was.

You might feel caught in that same situation. When we

> AS LONG AS THE ENEMY CAN KEEP YOU STUCK IN WHO YOU USED TO BE, HE DOES NOT HAVE TO WORRY ABOUT THE MIRACLE YOU HAVE BECOME.

are becoming someone new and feel God doing something in our lives, we need to fully step into it. And yet too often we fear that people are going to hold us in that place where we started, so we end up holding ourselves captive there and don't let ourselves actually be free. Christian had to let go of who he had been to fully step into who he was becoming.

The Bible says when you die with Christ, when you're baptized, or whenever you give your life to Jesus, the old self is gone and a new self has come (2 Corinthians 5:17). "We were buried therefore with him by baptism into death, in order that, just as Christ was raised from the dead by the glory of the Father, we too might walk in newness of life" (Romans 6:4 ESV).

Baptism symbolizes that you are burying your old self and are washed clean under Jesus' blood, and when you come back up you are new. You are no longer the version of you that people used to know. You're starting a new life. When Christian gave his life to Jesus, he was letting go of his old self and becoming someone new. So, of course, he was going to act differently than he used to. That's how it should be. That is the power of the gospel. Christian experienced exactly what the Bible describes: he became new.

I have heard people comment that God does not seem to perform miracles like He did in biblical times. Many in today's culture question if God is even capable of performing miracles. Maybe that comes from not seeing any of them for themselves. Maybe that comes from never asking for a miracle. Or maybe they did ask once, and God did not provide the miracle they were expecting, and they are upset because they don't understand why.

Regardless of where you stand on God being a miracle-working God, I have to say that I believe with my whole heart that He was and still is because I have seen it. And no, I have not seen a mountain physically move, but when someone goes from old to new and from dead to alive, that is a miracle.

Jesus gives us the opportunity to embrace Him in His death and resurrection and become a new self. Don't doubt that this miracle can happen for you. You get to walk with Jesus and live a better life.

Before the Rooster Crows

The necessity of moving forward is shown in the lives of so many in the Bible. We see it in every disciple as Jesus challenged them to leave everything behind and follow Him. We see it in the life of Paul, previously known as Saul, a murderer of Christians who went on to write half of the New Testament after having an encounter with Jesus. We also see it in the Old Testament when God used Moses, who had to press past the past in his own life, to lead all the Israelites out of Egypt to the promised land.

Moving forward is important in order to continue on with any story, especially God's story. I have heard it said before that "if you're not dead, God's not done."

I want us to focus specifically on Peter's journey of moving forward. The night before Jesus was taken to be crucified, He sat with His disciples for the Last Supper. He began to tell of what was about to happen, and the disciples were in complete denial. Peter especially was not taking this news of what was to come very well.

"Jesus said to him, 'Truly, I tell you, this very night, before the rooster crows, you will deny me three times.' Peter said to him, 'Even if I must die with you, I will not deny you!' And all the disciples said the same" (Matthew 26:34–35 ESV).

Yet hours later, sitting at a charcoal fire, Peter denied Jesus three times.

"Now Simon Peter was standing and warming himself. So they said to him, 'You also are not one of his disciples, are you?' He denied it and said, 'I am not.' One of the servants of the high priest, a relative of the man whose ear Peter had cut off, asked, 'Did I not see you in the garden with him?' Peter again denied it, and at once a rooster crowed" (John 18:25–27 ESV).

Words he couldn't take back, words that hurt someone else. He was one of Jesus' best friends and had literally said just the night before that he would give his life before he denied Jesus. Yet at that charcoal fire when he was in a moment of uncertainty and doubt, he denied Him. Jesus was crucified soon after, before they had a chance to talk again. The Bible says that Peter wept when the rooster crowed, as he realized what he had done and felt the magnitude of his mistake (Matthew 26:75).

ASK YOURSELF:

Do you feel you've done something too bad to have a relationship with the Lord?

Let's go back for a minute so we can see where Jesus and Peter's relationship began. First off, do you remember the story of the guy who said, "We have found the Messiah"? That guy was Peter's brother, Andrew. As soon as Andrew met Jesus, he introduced Him to Peter.

Peter and Andrew were fishermen, and one day Jesus walked up to them and called them to follow Him. "While walking by the Sea of Galilee, he saw two brothers, Simon (who is called Peter) and Andrew his brother, casting a net into the sea, for they were fishermen. And he said to them, 'Follow me, and I will make you fishers of men.' Immediately they left their nets and followed him" (Matthew 4:18–20 ESV).

It has always been remarkable to me that these men would drop all they knew, their very livelihood, to follow Jesus. Their lives as they knew it paled in comparison to the call of Jesus in that moment. He basically said, "Drop that life of fishing because I am going to give you a way to fish with a purpose. You will no longer fish for fish, but you will fish for men." This launched a friendship and ministry that changed the lives of countless men, women, and children and saved many souls.

Peter and Jesus had an incredible time together in the years that they fished for men, but after Jesus died, Peter did not know how to move forward. So, like many of us do in the face of uncertainty, he went back to what he had always known: fishing for fish. He gave up on the idea that his life had meaning. How could it after what he had done in denying Jesus?

Days after Peter watched his friend and Savior die on a cross, he was out fishing with six other disciples when a man appeared. The man called out to Peter and the other men, asking if they had any fish. They said no, and He told them to cast their net on the other side of the boat. When they did this they could not even pull up the net because of how many fish they had. In that moment they realized that the man was the Lord! Peter could not even hold his excitement; he jumped in the water and swam to meet up with Jesus.

It strikes me that as they were fishing that day, as they stepped back into the old habit of what they used to do before they found their purpose in Jesus, they were not catching anything. I feel like it is the same for us. When we experience the goodness of God and we see the new creation we could become, it is almost impossible to go back to how it was before and find any kind of real enjoyment. The things that used to make us laugh don't make us laugh anymore; the things that brought us pleasure just leave us with guilt; the things that used to create a sense of accomplishment don't fill our souls.

Once Christian tasted the goodness and fullness of God, there was no going back for him. Shotgunning a beer on a balcony to get drunk as fast as possible would not give him the life he knew was out there for him to live.

The Charcoal Fire

When Jesus showed up on the scene and Peter reached Him after swimming to shore, Jesus did something so human. He invited Peter to have breakfast. And guess where they sat? Around a charcoal fire. In that moment, the shame of Peter's past could have resurfaced, because this was basically a screenshot of his greatest mistake, yet Jesus used that moment to redeem the mistake.

> When they had finished breakfast, Jesus said to Simon Peter, "Simon, son of John, do you love me more than these?" He said to him, "Yes, Lord; you know that I love you." He said to him, "Feed my lambs." He said to him a second time, "Simon, son of John, do you love me?" He said to him, "Yes, Lord; you know that I love you." He said to him, "Tend my sheep." He said to him the third time, "Simon, son of John, do you love me?" Peter was grieved because he said to him the third time, "Do you love me?" and he said to him, "Lord, you know everything; you know that I love you." Jesus said to him, "Feed my sheep." (John 21:15–17 ESV)

In the very same setting where Peter had denied Jesus, Jesus gave him the opportunity for redemption. In this conversation Jesus asked, "Do you love me?" three times. He redeemed the three times Peter had denied Him by letting Peter affirm that he loved Him, and then He reminded Peter that he still had a purpose.

I think this is where a lot of people let their past stop them from stepping into their future. I have spoken to people from all different walks of life—college campuses, juvenile centers, prisons, churches, and even packed arenas—and so often I hear the question, "Do you think God still loves me? Because I have done a lot of wrong in my life." People are desperate to know if there is still hope for them after the choices they have made.

As sad as it makes me to see them wrestle with this question, I understand. For too long the church has made people feel this way. It has highlighted their worst mistakes and made them feel guilt and shame. It has convinced them if they are not "perfect," there is no place for them there. I believe it has also contributed to causing people to feel as though they do not have a purpose.

This is why we feel the need to cover up anything bad we have done, when in reality we don't need to hide it; we need to repent and move on. If we cannot be real and repentant in the church, then where can we be? Don't we all know that none of us are perfect and we all fall short of the glory of God (Romans 3:23)? Maybe we have forgotten that because of how perfect we all portray ourselves to be on social media.

Everyone posts their highlight reel and even that is filtered. Portraying our lives as perfect has made us think that our lives actually have to be perfect, and if they aren't, then we aren't good enough. We put an impossible standard of perfection on our lives because that's the image we have created for ourselves or have seen someone else show off. We take a hundred pictures and then choose the one with the best angle, filter it just right, craft the perfect words for a caption, and then want people to think our life looks just like the filtered one. Sometimes we even trick ourselves into believing that it does, when in reality it looks like the ninety-nine others. And because we didn't think the ninety-nine other pictures could get a like, how can we expect to love ourselves with all the flaws and mistakes that are simply part of being a real human?

In this story of Jesus and Peter eating breakfast around a charcoal fire, it amazes me that Peter was not the one asking the question to Jesus: "Do you still love me after I made this huge mistake?" He was not doubting himself because of how imperfect he had been. After denying Jesus three times and giving up on all they had worked for on earth, you would think that when Peter saw Jesus, he would fall to his knees and feel so unworthy of His presence. (That's how I've felt at times.) You would expect him to hide in the boat for fear of what Jesus would think. You would guess Peter would sit at breakfast anxiously wondering if there was any way Jesus could still love him after what he had done, and if He would ever be willing to be in a relationship with him again.

But this was not at all what happened. Peter did not hide in the boat; he jumped out of it. Peter did not hesitate to eat with Jesus; he sat there and enjoyed a meal. Peter did not ask Jesus if

He still loved him. He knew Jesus loved him because Jesus came back for him. (Interestingly enough, Jesus asked Peter if *he* still loved *Him*.) I have to believe that the reason Peter did not feel the need to ask Jesus if He still loved him is because that truth was just wildly obvious.

I want you to know, friends, that God's love for you is established. You don't have to try to be perfect, you don't have to craft the perfect thing to say, and you don't have to hide your flaws. Romans 5:8 says, "God shows his love for us in that while we were still sinners, Christ died for us" (ESV)! While you were a sinner, Jesus chose to die for you. It was proven at the cross, but it wasn't finished at the cross. He then came back to life, breaking the power of sin and death over your life, and He now welcomes you into a new life and an eternal hope.

We don't have to wonder if God loves us. He loved us so much that He sent His Son to die for us to save us. Not only that, but He sent His Spirit out as a daily reminder, to meet us where we are and remind us of His love. He is inviting us into a life with Him and a hope of eternal glory.

Yes—God loves you!

Despite what you have done, He loves you!

Despite who you were, He loves you!

Despite who others know you to be, He loves you!

He does not want you to sit in the boat another day coming up empty-handed, dwelling on who you used to be. He is ready for you to become who He has called you to be. But you have to be willing to sit back down at the fire and let Him redeem all that is in you.

Just like Peter had to face the past, so did Christian, and so did I. Can it feel really hard? Yes, absolutely. The past is not only embarrassing but also painful. The beautiful thing is, you don't have to just walk away and pretend it never happened. Jesus can handle hearing about it and is able to redeem it, so that when you look at the charcoal fire you no longer see your failure. Instead, you see your victory in Him. When Christian looks back at his past, he doesn't have to feel shameful; he can be reminded of how loved he is. He no longer has to see his weakness; he can see God's strength. He does not have to look at just his story; he can see his testimony.

ASK YOURSELF:
What word have you been declaring over your past that you need Jesus to redeem? Is it *failure*, *lost*, *dirty*, *weak*, *sinner* . . . ? Let God give you a new word today.

It is a huge temptation to just keep the past in the past, but as long as you feel like you are hiding something you will live as a slave to the fear of being found out. Don't hide it. Embrace it with the One who can redeem it. The very thing Christian used to be scared to share with his own parents is the thing he now willingly shares with everyone he meets. He'd been so scared to tell them about his mistakes, just like we can be scared to tell God about our own, but my in-laws showed such a picture of how God responds when we confess our past sins to Him—with forgiveness and love.

After Peter had a moment of reestablishing the love he had for Jesus, Jesus reestablished his purpose. He went back to the words He had challenged Peter with at the beginning of their journey. He said, "Follow me" (John 21:19). Peter's purpose was not over because of his past. Jesus did not want to lose His follower.

Peter continued to follow Jesus even after Jesus ascended back into heaven. In fact, he was such a strong follower of Jesus that he actually started the church. Peter preached the sermon at Pentecost (Acts 2)! Everything we know as the church was started because of Peter and that conversation that he had with Jesus. Can you imagine if Peter had let his past stop him from stepping into his future? I don't know what my life would be right now if Peter had not pressed past the past. I also don't know what my life would be if Christian had not pressed past the past. Peter's willingness to accept redemption, to let go of his old self, and to move forward restored as a new man became the basis for the entire creation of our church.

No matter what your past looks like, or what everyone saw you do, or maybe even what you posted on social media that people know as your past, you are never too far gone to become who you know you can be. It does not matter what your feed in the past looked like or what's in your tagged photos from the weekends. Just because you made mistakes does not mean that Jesus will love you less. Those broken places can become the perfect places to meet with Jesus and receive His love, places where He can transform your whole life.

But remember, just because He loves you does not mean He will let you sit comfortably where you are. "What shall we say, then? Shall we go on sinning so that grace may increase? By no means! We are those who have died to sin; how can we live in it any longer?" (Romans 6:1–2). Jesus has something better for you. A way forward. Now you have to be willing to walk on.

YOUR PAST DOESN'T HAVE TO HOLD YOU BACK. NO MATTER WHAT YOU'VE DONE OR WHO YOU'VE BEEN, YOU CAN BE A NEW CREATION IN JESUS TODAY.

are you following your truth or *the* truth?

You are to follow no man further than he follows Christ.
JOHN COLLINS[1]

WHEN CHRISTIAN AND I WERE DATING WE WERE CON-stantly in communication about where we were and what we were doing, because we dated long distance and always wanted to keep each other in the loop. Well, one night he went to a friend's going-away party. That friend happened to be a girl, and Christian happened to forget to tell me that he was going.

About three weeks later, I was on Instagram and saw a picture from the party—with Christian and his female friend. I was pretty surprised that my boyfriend had his arm around another girl I didn't know and was at a party I didn't know about. Let's just say I was a little confused and not very happy about it. When I asked Christian about it, he responded by saying, "I told her not to post that." You can imagine that this was not the response I was looking for, and I'm just going to be real with y'all: I was mad.

Following Your Own Truth

Literally months after this conversation, I still could not get past it. It really hurt my trust in Christian, and I just kept replaying those words over and over: "I told her not to post it." As if all this would have been okay if I had never found out. I questioned Christian many times as to why he asked her not to post it, because that made it seem like he was hiding something. It really bothered me for a while, but finally I knew I had to drop it if I was going to move on, and I had to forgive him.

More months went by and one day I woke up from a nap to find Christian sitting beside me. With a shaky voice and tears in his eyes, he told me, "I lied."

"What?" I was so confused as to what he was talking about, because again, this was months later.

He then said, "I didn't tell her not to post the picture. I only said that because I thought it would be better if you thought I had wished she hadn't posted it. But the truth is, I just never thought it would get posted. I went to that party for fifteen minutes with my guy friends to tell her bye because she was a good friend of mine, and we took a picture, but that is it. I'm sorry I didn't just say this months ago. I was just too embarrassed. It has bothered me ever since."

The truth in this situation was so simple, and if he would have told me the truth early on, it would have been nothing to even discuss. But a little lie sent us into months of confusion and a couple of headaches that we did not need, all because the truth was hard to say.

The truth is usually simple until we try to create our own. Normally when we try to create our own truth we complicate things so much that we forget what the truth even is. I see this happening in our day with the Word of God and our fleshly desires. Remember that game we talked about, Two Truths and a Lie? Well, nowadays it looks like this: "I didn't get my work done today. I am not where I want to be. I am worthless." Yes, the truth is you did not get your work done. And maybe you are not where you want to be, but that does not mean that you are worthless. That little lie of worthlessness mixed in with some truth can take you down a dark road.

Here's another set of two truths and a lie I've seen as well:

> THE TRUTH IS USUALLY SIMPLE UNTIL WE TRY TO CREATE OUR OWN.

"I love my best friend. She is so beautiful. I must be a lesbian." Yes, it's true that you love your best friend, because she is your best friend. Also, she may be very beautiful. But just because the first two things are true does not make the last one true. When you try to figure out the truth by creating your own truth, you are just distancing yourself from *the truth*, which only leads to more confusion.

Sometimes it looks like this: "My jeans didn't fit today. I woke up with such bad acne. I am ugly." You start to believe the one lie mixed in with the truth, and the next thing you know, you believe you are unlovable. That lie can lead you down a path you don't want to go on.

> WHEN YOU TRY TO FIGURE OUT THE TRUTH BY CREATING YOUR OWN TRUTH, YOU ARE JUST DISTANCING YOURSELF FROM *THE TRUTH*, WHICH ONLY LEADS TO MORE CONFUSION.

Don't listen to the lies that come up in your thoughts. They'll only bring you confusion and point you away from your true identity. You could go on a journey for the rest of your life trying to find and create a truth that will allow you to feel seen, known, and loved, but I want you to know that there is already a truth that says that, and it is in the Word of God. I don't want you to wake up from a nap in years to come still confused as to how you got there and say, "Why didn't someone just tell me the truth?"

ASK YOURSELF:

What are some lies that are getting mixed in with truth in your thought life?

Following *the* Truth

I remember the first time I went to a Taylor Swift concert. She was coming to a city about an hour and a half away from where I live. Growing up in small-town Louisiana, if someone like Taylor Swift was coming anywhere near, it was a really big deal. You definitely made sure to show up. We got our tickets and made the trip to see T. Swift in person. When we got there we were getting situated in our seats, and as everyone else sat down, I was strategically making my move to get the aisle seat, because I had heard that at one point in the concert Taylor would run from stage A to stage B. This would mean that she just might have to run right past us. And she did! I remember as she ran by in her fringe dress, I reached out, hoping to just touch the fringe of her garment.

When Taylor Swift ran by that night and I reached out to touch her as she passed, I was hyped—I'm not going to lie. She even threw me her guitar pick. I was really thriving in my preteens.

But I have to be honest with you: that moment did not change my life. Nor did it really offer any kind of lasting enjoyment or blessing. Because the thing is, no matter how famous a person is, it doesn't mean they are any more important than you are.

There's only one famous person who has ever lived that,

when you touch the fringe of His garment, you're healed. No other garment will heal you. No one but Jesus Christ can truly change you, bringing you from death to life. Jesus' fame is the only fame worth running after and reaching out to.

Jesus was very famous when He lived on earth. Mark 6:53–56 says:

> When they had crossed over [the sea], they reached the land of Gennesaret and anchored at the shore. They got out of the boat and immediately people recognized Him, and ran throughout that surrounding countryside and began to carry around on their mats those who were sick, to any place where they heard He was. And wherever He came into villages, or cities, or the countryside, they were laying the sick in the market places and pleading with Him [to allow them] just to touch the fringe (tassel with a blue cord) of His robe; and all who touched it were healed. (AMP)

Jesus was immediately recognized. Crowds of people ran to Him in cities and villages and countrysides. Everybody who had heard the name of Jesus wanted to be where He was. They wanted to touch the fringe of His garment. Sounds like how we treat famous people, doesn't it? But those who ran to Him were truly healed.

I believe that our generation craves truth, direction, and guidance, but too often, for the sake of growing the church, we hear a watered-down version of the gospel that simplifies the message and makes it more palatable to the masses. We hear things like, "All you have to do is say, 'I love you, Jesus.' Simple as that!" And while, yes, God does love when you acknowledge your love for Him and that's a really nice thing to think about, that's not what the Bible says. In fact, this whole approach to the gospel message is more harmful than it is helpful.

In a recent survey of pastors in the US, 72 percent cited "watered down gospel teachings" as the biggest threat to strong discipleship. It should come as no surprise then that a majority of pastors (66 percent) recognized our "culture's shift to a secular age" as a major concern for the church today.[2]

Blending Truth and Love

God loves us and there is no doubt about it. But God also has a purpose for our lives, and it involves more than just saying we believe He is who He says He is. God's Word says that even the demons believe (James 2:19), but really following Jesus involves more than that.

Matt Chandler has discussed how taking away God's wrath means taking away His love.[3] I agree with him. Just as a parent, out of love, has wrath when they see sin come into their child's life, so does God. The way of sin is not the way God created us to live. When we step outside of His way, it always leads to pain, confusion, and hurt, the opposite of the abundant life He has for us. If God did not care about your sin, then He really would not care about your life.

If we're still saying, "You do you," or, "You live your truth," then no wonder we're not getting the fruit the Bible promises us. A lot of people who claim to be Christians are not living in *the* truth, which is why they don't understand why they're not happy, why they're not free from their sin, why they're not joyful, why they don't have peace.

I have been asking God a lot of questions lately about how to follow Him in the days that we are facing. I'm not talking about just following Him like I've hit the Follow button, see His updates when they scroll across my page, and like them every once in a while. I'm talking about truly following Him in the way that His Word says, not just in a way that is comfortable for me.

Even though I am confident in His Word being the truth, I struggle to find the words to say to be the light of the world in the midst of a culture waiting to cancel people. We also live in a society in which the truth is whatever makes people feel the most comfortable and the most "true to themselves." I wrestle with the desire to speak up but question if it's right to speak if people only listen to a headline taken out of context.

The other day I wrote a question for God in my journal, and I want to share it with you. I said, "Jesus, You were friends with sinners. You reclined at the table for meals with people who were so different than You. Because You are the truth, I know that You were always truthful, so how did You get the sinners to stay at the table? How are You both truth and love?"

I pondered that question for days as I hesitated to write this last chapter on what it means to follow Jesus, and then as I worshiped one night, I figured out an answer: Jesus was a friend.

God did not just shout out words from the atmosphere down

to all His followers, saying, "This is the way to get to Me." Instead, He sent Jesus to become a friend and to show us the way. A friend tells the truth out of love and does not guide you in the wrong direction. And the one being helped does not feel judged, but rather loved that his friend cares enough to get him on the right path. I hope as we close

> YOU WERE ALWAYS TRUTHFUL, SO HOW DID YOU GET THE SINNERS TO STAY AT THE TABLE? HOW ARE YOU BOTH TRUTH AND LOVE?

out on a rather challenging truth about following Jesus that you will leave feeling loved, because you and I have become friends.

I also realized another answer to my question. Not everyone did stay at the table. A lot of sinners never would have entered the house where Jesus was staying. The fact is, not everyone wants to hear the truth. Some people would rather have their friends say what makes them feel better than tell the truth that may hurt to hear (but heal in the long run).

I believe the truth—and I mean the real truth, no matter how uncomfortable it can be to hear—will set you free.

In trying to create a bigger church, we're creating a weaker church and a really loose idea of Christianity. We have to be confident that the Bible teaches what it teaches for a reason—not to scare people away, but to truly love people in full truth. I don't want the watered-down gospel. I want the power of the real thing! I want the thing that makes dead people alive again!

Now, we can't know if church leaders or other influencers are truly sharing God's message from His Word if we ourselves don't know what the Word says. The incredible thing is, we actually have the Word of God. It's in our hands, on our phones; it's just a click away at any moment. We don't need to follow a pastor or influencer to know the truth. We can read it and see what God says about death and life, the good life and the sinful life, what He says about you, His promises for you, His sending His Son for you. It's all there.

I always find it fascinating when someone tells me that they don't have time to read their Bible or spend time with God, and yet they wish they knew Scripture more. But that same person can quote every line from their favorite artist's last album, do every move to the latest TikTok trend, or tell you everything about their favorite influencer's life. We don't have a lack of time. It is a matter of who we're obsessed with and who we worship. Who are you really following?

ASK YOURSELF:
Who or what are you truly following?

Following Jesus

Jesus actually addressed this idea of how to follow Him in Matthew 16:24. I am going to put it here in the Amplified

Version so we can really understand what He was saying: "If anyone wishes to follow Me [as My disciple], he must deny himself [set aside selfish interests], and take up his cross [expressing a willingness to endure whatever may come] and follow Me [believing in Me, conforming to My example in living and, if need be, suffering or perhaps dying because of faith in Me]."

When Jesus talked about following Him, He didn't sugarcoat it at all. He didn't say, "Follow Me, it'll be great. You're going to live an amazing life and I will pour my blessings on you financially." Instead, it's a much more realistic message: "Follow Me. It will probably be hard. People will probably persecute you and even hate you, but remember they hated Me first. I will be with you and give you strength to endure. Follow Me because I can give you eternal life."

Jesus straight up said, "If you want to follow Me, you have to deny yourself and set aside your selfish interests." This is such an unpopular message for our day. You hear all day long, "You do you, boo." You see so many celebrities even preaching the opposite message of the gospel, saying, "Live your truth," or, "Wake up and choose you today."

Our culture preaches to choose you, to do whatever makes you smile, happy, or comfortable. And many times we hear leaders in the church saying the same thing because no one wants to upset or offend anyone—or maybe just because we are all so ingrained in this culture that we can't see the lies in the truths either.

The problem is, that is not the message the gospel preaches. It does not say, "Choose you"; it says, "Choose Jesus." It does not say, "Do what makes you comfortable or happy"; it says, "No matter what, endure what is to come—even unto death—if it means choosing Jesus."

Jesus doesn't preach this message because He is against you; Jesus preaches this message because *He is for you.* You have to remember God created you, He formed you, He knows you. Jesus chose you, He lived for you, and He died for you. And He just might know more about you than you do. We don't always know what is best for ourselves, but our Creator does.

Think about when you were a little kid. You would want something so badly and ask your parents to give it to you, and they would say no. You would get mad and complain and cry, wanting your way, letting your feelings be your guide, wanting to live your truth. Meanwhile, your parents could see what was best for you. When they told you no, it was not them going against you. It was actually them being for you.

It's the same with God our Father. He is the perfect parent, the parent who knows every hair on your head and loves you so much He would die for you. What you have viewed as Him being against you is actually His loving-kindness for you.

God Sees You

I was watching *American Idol* the other night, which is one of my favorite shows. A girl walked out on the stage, clearly so nervous to sing and not believing in her own talent. But her mom had seen something really special in her and had encouraged her to go on the show. She sang and she was amazing. She kept going further and further in the competition and yet her confidence did not grow. Finally Katy Perry looked her in the eye and said, "Believe in your mom. She can see you."

Her words struck me in that moment because many of us struggle to believe God has His best for us since we cannot see Him. But Katy Perry had a point. It was not being able to see her mom that should have helped her confidence grow. It was that her mom could see her—her talent, her ability, her voice, and her life. It is not about you needing to *see* God to be affirmed in who you are; it is that He sees you. Trust that He knows what is best for you. Trust that when you deny your own selfish desires and choose His way, it will actually be the greatest thing for your life and lead you to the one to come.

ASK YOURSELF:

Do you believe that God can see you better than anyone else can? What do you think He sees when He looks at you? Do you believe He affirms you? How would you live differently if your confidence was based on His view of you?

The Cost

You might be thinking, *Wow, following Jesus is costly.* You may just want to continue aimlessly following celebrities, trends, and methods through endless clicks and scrolls, thinking you will avoid the price. But I want you to consider: Is the cost of following worldly temptations really free? Or are you actually paying the ultimate price? Are you actually counting a greater cost by following and devoting your time to things that are essentially meaningless to saving your soul? "What does it profit a man to gain the whole world and forfeit his soul?" (Mark 8:36 ESV).

Is what you're following costing you your peace of mind, your purpose, or your freedom to live confidently?

Everything has a price. The question is, is it worth the cost? Maybe you remember the stats we talked about in chapter 1: 40 million adults have an anxiety disorder, 28.8 million will have an eating disorder in their lifetime, and 16.2 million adults have had a major depressive episode. It seems clear that what we have been following is not leading us to peace, joy, hope, love, and life. It is leading us down roads of anxiety, depression, self-hate, and sin.

But there is *hope*. There is a way. There is a truth. There is a life.

I have tried both ways. I've ended up as one of these statistics myself. I have lived in anxiety and insecurity, but I moved forward. I have found that following Jesus has truly led me to the life I desire to live and an eternal life to come. Who are you going to follow?

DENY YOURSELF AND FOLLOW
JESUS. THE REWARD OF HAVING
HIM IN YOUR WORLD WILL
OUTWEIGH EVERY COST.

yes or no?

IF YOU'VE EVER PLAYED TWENTY QUESTIONS, YOU know it's a guessing game where one player thinks of a person, place, or thing and then has the other player guess what they are thinking as they answer questions with either a yes or a no. It can be hilarious as imaginations run wild—especially because there's always way more you don't know than you do know.

Here's something you really *need* to know. And guessing isn't going to be good enough because it's the ultimate Q & A.

Ready?

Have you told God that He is the One you want to follow?

This goes beyond reading about God, or even talking about Him; it's a decision to have a personal relationship with Him that is not a list of religious dos and don'ts.

All throughout this book I've presented who I know God and His Son, Jesus, to be—not just from what I learned as a kid but what has been proven to be true in my life as an adult. And with it comes an open invitation from God Himself, who says, "Come to me" (Matthew 11:28).

Maybe you've read this whole book, or maybe you've just flipped to the back to see what's here. Whether you end here or begin here, I'm glad you *are* here, because this is the most important thing we could talk about together.

There's a simple prayer you can pray.

Dear Jesus, I know that I am a sinner, and I ask for Your forgiveness. I believe You died for my sins and rose from the dead. I turn from my sins and invite You to come into my heart and life. I want to trust and follow You as my Lord and Savior.

This is your moment of repentance. Romans 10:9 says, "If you declare with your mouth, 'Jesus is Lord,' and believe in your heart that God raised him from the dead, you will be saved."

You might not feel any different, but the gospel is about facts, not feelings. If you have put your faith in Christ, then you have been forgiven, and He has come into your life. Just remember this is not about simply saying the words, but about truly believing in your heart.

Okay, so now what?

Here are four things that will help you grow in this new relationship. It's called Time to Get REAL:

Read the Bible: Start with the Gospel of John.

Encounter the Author: Talk to God every day in prayer.

Attend church: Get plugged into a local Bible-teaching church.

Let others know: Tell people about what God has done in your life.[1]

I even encourage you to be born again through baptism and make a public declaration of your faith so that those around you can watch you lay down your old self and step into the new.

While we've talked a lot about following in this book, especially following Jesus, you can know this with certainty—He will always be your ultimate follow!

follower
reset

FOLLOWING PEOPLE ON SOCIAL MEDIA, KEEPING UP
with your favorite online influencers, regularly reading a blog,
having a friend you consider a role model—all these things can
be awesome. The internet can be a great place to connect with
your friends, find the latest trends, and even start a business! So
the last thing I want to do with this book is put people off the
internet and social media or tell them to stop interacting with
people in enjoyable ways.

However, I will say that from time to time, you need to
answer some key questions:

- Who are you following and how is it impacting you?
- Which voices are speaking into your life the most?

- How much time do you spend following people online versus building real-life connections?
- Which people cause you to think, *I wish that was my life?*

Why do these issues matter? Friend, if you're not paying attention to them, you might navigate yourself completely off track from where God intends you to be. It's like relying on a compass that is off by one degree.

That's why I've included this Follower Reset. We all need a reminder to take a few minutes to check in with ourselves and evaluate who we are following.

If you feel confident about who you are following, great. If you have amazing voices speaking into your life—both online and in your real life—and you're in a solid place, I'm proud of you. If you're not sure if the impact of who you are following is always healthy or you absolutely know they aren't (trust me, I've been there), work through the Follower Assessment below.

Ask yourself these important *what, when, where, who,* and *why* questions. Write down your answers on this page, in a journal, or even on a note-taking phone app. But be sure to write them down. This will help you really think through who you are following and what needs to change. Keep in mind that the people we follow are not always online, so be sure to look at your life fully, not just your social media habits.

We will set goals after the assessment, so be honest with yourself during this first part. Just write down the facts, then we will go from there!

Follower Assessment

WHO are the loudest voices in my life?

You don't have to list every voice—perhaps start with the top ten. Who are the people you pay closest attention to? These can be people online or in your real life. Think through the different areas of your life: friends, family members, pastors, influencers on social media, professors, professional athletes, coworkers, etc.

WHAT platforms are influencing my life?

What apps are you using? What do you watch on TV and YouTube? What podcasts do you listen to? List every social media app you have an account for, every streaming service you have on your TV, the main podcasts and YouTube channels you listen to or watch, and any other platform you spend time on.

WHERE am when I let these voices and platforms influence my life?

Think about the locations throughout your day—at your home, on your campus, at your job, in your car, where you spend your lunch break, etc.

WHEN do I find myself giving time and space to following these individuals?

How much time each week do you spend letting these voices directly speak into your life? Perhaps you check your phone first thing in the morning, or you find yourself spending hours in the evening watching certain programs on TV or YouTube. Do you think you're on certain platforms too much? Do you neglect your to-do list to be around certain people or places?

WHY do I follow these individuals?

This is a big question, but it's important to think about. Are you seeking something specific from following these individuals? Perhaps it is to feel inspired by what they are saying or doing. Maybe they have great business tips or techniques. You might be following them because you like their fashion or you wish your life looked like theirs. Whatever the reason, be honest with yourself and take time to truly reflect here. You will probably have different reasons for different people and influences.

Follower Goals

Now that you have a clear picture of who you are following, does anything about it bother you? Chances are this Follower Assessment has left you wondering if you should make some changes.

Use the next questions to set some goals for changing your habits. Keep in mind that you don't have to do all of these at once! Just take small steps toward each goal over the next few weeks and see what happens. And know that I am preaching this message to myself more than anyone. You aren't alone here.

WHO do I want to influence my life?

Which ones encourage and inspire you? What relationships in your life point you toward Jesus and teach you more about Him? Who are the people who make you feel good about yourself? Those might be the ones you want to keep following.

Now, who does the opposite in your life? Which relationships fill your mind with gossip or judgmental thoughts? Which ones convince you to buy things you don't need? Which ones make you wish you were a certain way that does not align with what you believe? You don't need this negativity in your life. I can promise you that these relationships are not worth following. You will find nothing life-giving or glorifying to God by following them.

WHAT apps, platforms, podcasts, shows, etc. do I need to get rid of, and which ones do I want to keep speaking into my life?

Do some of these voices lead you to mindsets and feelings you don't want to have, while others leave you feeling happy and encouraged? Do you have too many voices, apps, and influencers speaking into your life? Determine which ones are worth keeping and which ones you need to unsubscribe from.

WHERE is the best place in my life to engage with these influences?

What patterns did you notice when you looked at where you consume most of your content? Where is a good place for you to check social media in your home or workplace that won't lead to endless scrolling? What do you want to listen to in your car when you drive? What new boundaries do you need to set in this area?

WHEN is the best time for me to allow these influences in my life?

Do you need to set some new time boundaries based on your notes above? Maybe this means giving less time in your day or week to personal relationships that are negatively impacting you. Perhaps this means spending more time in nature, with family, or with a life-giving small group from church. It could also be a social media or screen time goal, such as limiting your scrolling to just a few times throughout the day that would make sense for your schedule.

WHY do I want to follow these people, both in my real life and on these platforms?

Perhaps you need to change the reason you are on social media, or maybe the assessment you just did made you realize you don't really have a reason. Knowing your purpose will help you narrow down who to follow, which platforms to be on, and how to interact with them.

I know this has given you a lot to think about! It may seem overwhelming at first, but asking myself these same questions has really helped me. Recognizing who I am following and setting some boundaries about when and how often I allow these voices in my life has allowed me to engage with the people I want to have in my life. When we become intentional about who is influencing us, we can become better influencers.

acknowledgments

CHRISTIAN, YOU ARE MY BIGGEST CHEERLEADER.
Thank you for rejoicing with me during the writing process and crying with me at times too.

Thank you to my Live Original team. Without you, it doesn't happen.

Mom and Dad, you set the best example for following Jesus. Thank you for continuously pushing me to think more deeply.

Thank you to Brandi Bowles and the UTA team for making dreams happen.

Thank you to the incredible W team for making this book better and better. You made a challenging writing project a very enjoyable process.

Debbie Wickwire, you are a godsend. Your impact on the world is larger than most will ever realize, and I'm grateful I got the opportunity to work with you.

Lastly, to mentors like Louie and Shelley Giglio, Jennie Allen, Christine Caine, Priscilla Shirer, and Alex Seeley: thank you for showing me what it looks like to lead a crowd to Jesus.

notes

CHAPTER 1: WHO IS INFLUENCING YOU?

1. John C. Maxwell, *The 21 Irrefutable Laws of Leadership: Follow Them and People Will Follow You* (Nashville, TN: HarperCollins, 1998, 2007), 51.

2. Jennifer Wagner, "Infographic: Millennials vs Gen-Z Social Media Usage," Ignite Social Media, July 31, 2020, https://www.ignitesocialmedia.com/social-media-marketing/infographic-millennials-vs-gen-z-social-media-usage/.

3. "Common Sense Census: Media Use by Tweens and Teens, 2019," Common Sense Media, accessed July 15, 2021, https://www.commonsensemedia.org/Media-use-by-tweens-and-teens-2019-infographic.

4. Salman Aslam, "Facebook by the Numbers: Stats, Demographics & Fun Facts," Omnicore, January 4, 2021, https://www.omnicoreagency.com/facebook-statistics/. Cristos Goodrow, "You Know What's Cool? A Billion Hours," YouTube Official Blog, February 27, 2017, https://blog.youtube/news-and-events/you-know-whats-cool-billion-hours/. Andrew Hutchinson, "Snapchat Now Serving 10 Billion Video Views Per Day—the

Evolution of the Ghost," Social Media Today, April 29, 2016, https://www.socialmediatoday.com/social-networks/snapchat-now-serving-10-billion-video-views-day-evolution-ghost.

5. Salman Aslam, "Instagram by the Numbers: Stats, Demographics & Fun Facts," Omnicore, January 3, 2021, https://www.omnicoreagency.com/instagram-statistics/.

6. Sudeep Srivastava, "52+ Striking Snapchat Statistics and Facts (2019–2020)," Appinventiv, updated September 17, 2020, https://appinventiv.com/blog/snapchat-app-statistics/.

7. Aleh Barysevich, "How Social Media Influence 71% Consumer Buying Decisions," Search Engine Watch, November 20, 2020, https://www.searchenginewatch.com/2020/11/20/how-social-media-influence-71-consumer-buying-decisions/.

8. "Average Time Spent Daily on Social Media (Latest 2020 Data): Time Spent on Social Media in a Lifetime," Broadband Search, accessed July 15, 2021, https://www.broadbandsearch.net/blog/average-daily-time-on-social-media#post-navigation-2.

9. Monica Anderson, "A Majority of Teens Have Experienced Some Form of Cyberbullying," Pew Research Center, September 27, 2018, https://www.pewresearch.org/internet/2018/09/27/a-majority-of-teens-have-experienced-some-form-of-cyberbullying/.

10. Anderson, "A Majority of Teens."

11. "Facts & Statistics," Anxiety and Depression Association of America, updated April 21, 2021, https://adaa.org/understanding-anxiety/facts-statistics.

12. Brandi Koskie, "Depression: Facts, Statistics, and You," Healthline, June 3, 2020, https://www.healthline.com/health/depression/facts-statistics-infographic#Types-of-depression.

13. Deloitte Access Economics, *The Social and Economic Cost of Eating Disorders in the United States of America: A Report for the Strategic Training Initiative for the Prevention of Eating Disorders and the Academy for Eating Disorders*, June 2020, https://www.hsph.harvard.edu/striped/report-economic-costs-of-eating-disorders/, quoted in "Eating Disorder Statistics," ANAD,

accessed July 15, 2021, https://anad.org/get-informed/about
-eating-disorders/eating-disorders-statistics/.

14. Deloitte Access Economics quoted in "Eating Disorder
Statistics," ANAD.

15. Tim Newman, "Anxiety in the West: Is It on the Rise?" Medical
News Today, September 5, 2018, https://www.medicalnewstoday
.com/articles/322877#Why-does-U.S.-society-breed-anxiety.

CHAPTER 2: WHAT ARE YOU SEEKING?

1. Ken Costa, *Know Your Why: Finding and Fulfilling Your Calling
in Life* (Nashville: Thomas Nelson, 2016), 86.

2. *The Oxford Pocket Dictionary of Current English*, s.v. "pure,"
Encyclopedia.com, accessed July 19, 2021, https://www
.encyclopedia.com/humanities/dictionaries-thesauruses-pictures
-and-press-releases/pure-0.

CHAPTER 3: HOW DO YOU GO FROM LIKED TO LOVED?

1. Timothy Keller and Kathy Keller, *The Meaning of Marriage:
Facing the Complexities of Commitment with the Wisdom of God*
(New York: Penguin Books, 2013), 101.

2. *Lexico US Dictionary*, s.v. "like," https://www.lexico.com/en
/definition/like.

3. Amanda MacMillan, "Why Instagram Is the Worst Social Media
for Mental Health," *TIME*, May 25, 2017, https://time.com
/4793331/instagram-social-media-mental-health/.

4. Jamie Leventhal, "How Removing 'Likes' from Instagram
Could Affect Our Mental Health," PBS News Hour, November
25, 2019, https://www.pbs.org/newshour/science/how-removing
-likes-from-instagram-could-affect-our-mental-health.

5. Kira E. Riehm, Kenneth A. Feder, Kayla N. Tormohlen, et al.,
"Associations Between Time Spent Using Social Media and
Internalizing and Externalizing Problems Among US Youth,"
JAMA Psychiatry 76, no. 12 (2019): 1266–73, https://jamanetwork
.com/journals/jamapsychiatry/article-abstract/2749480.

6. "How Social Media Addiction Affects Teenagers," Northwest Primary Care, accessed August 9, 2021, https://www.nwpc.com /social-media-addiction-affects-teenagers/.

7. Keller and Keller, *Meaning of Marriage*, 101.

CHAPTER 4: WHO ARE YOU COMPARING YOURSELF TO?

1. Christine Caine (@ChristineCaine), "When we compare ourselves or compete with one another, it works against what God intends for us," Twitter, August 7, 2020, 6:09 p.m., https:// twitter.com/christinecaine/status/1291874235921489920.

2. Christine Caine, "When we compare ourselves."

3. Christopher S. Baird, "Are There Any Parts of the Human Body That Get Oxygen Directly from the Air and Not from the Blood?" Science Questions with Surprising Answers, June 25, 2015, https://www.wtamu.edu/~cbaird/sq/2015/06/25/are-there -any-parts-of-the-human-body-that-get-oxygen-directly-from -the-air-and-not-from-the-blood/.

4. "Cornea Structure Layers and Function," University of Kansas Medical Center, accessed October 3, 2021, https://www.kumc .edu/Documents/ophthalmology/Cornea%20Structure%20 Layers%20and%20Function%20web.pdf.

5. "Cornea Structure Layers and Function." "Common Cornea Problems," WebMD, accessed October 12, 2021, https://www .webmd.com/eye-health/cornea-conditions-symptoms-treatments.

CHAPTER 5: WHY DO YOU WANT TO BE FAMOUS?

1. "Fred Rogers Hall of Fame Induction 1999," EMMYS, Television Academy, November 13, 2017, https://www.emmys.com/video /fred-rogers-hall-fame-induction-1999.

2. Russell Heimlich, "Gen Nexters Say Getting Rich Is Their Generation's Top Goal," Pew Research Center, January 23, 2007, https://www.pewresearch.org/fact-tank/2007/01/23/gen -nexters-say-getting-rich-is-their-generations-top-goal/.

3. Benedict Carey, "The Fame Motive," *New York Times*, August

22, 2006, https://www.nytimes.com/2006/08/22/health /psychology/22fame.html.

4. Christopher Osburn, "New Data Reveals Just How Desperately Millennials Want to Be Famous," Uproxx, January 25, 2017, https:// uproxx.com/life/millennials-desperately-want-to-be-famous/.

5. Sharon Jayson, "Survey: Young People Who Use Social Media Seek Fame," *USA Today*, April 18, 2013, https://www.usatoday.com/story /news/nation/2013/04/18/social-media-tweens-fame/2091199/.

6. Carey, "The Fame Motive."

7. The NAS Old Testament Hebrew Lexicon, s.v. "*bara*," Bible Study Tools, https://www.biblestudytools.com/lexicons/hebrew /nas/bara.html.

8. Larissa Rainey, "The Search for Purpose in Life: An Exploration of Purpose, the Search Process, and Purpose Anxiety," University of Pennsylvania Scholarly Columns, August 2014, 66, https:// repository.upenn.edu/cgi/viewcontent.cgi?article=1061&context =mapp_capstone.

9. Rainey, "The Search for Purpose in Life," 67.

10. Patrick L. Hill and Nicholas A. Turiano, "Purpose in Life as a Predictor of Mortality Across Adulthood," *Psychological Science* 25, no. 7 (July 2014): 1482–86, https://www.ncbi.nlm.nih.gov /pmc/articles/PMC4224996/.

11. Elaine Mead, "What Is 'Purpose Anxiety' and Do You Have It?" Healthline, June 1, 2020, https://www.healthline.com/health/what -is-purpose-anxiety-do-you-have-it#The-psychology-of-purpose.

12. Michael Todd (@iammiketodd), "All You Have Is All You Need. #thisisv1," video, 1:00, Facebook, September 18, 2019, https:// www.facebook.com/watch/?v=767002523733295.

13. Dr. Daniel Amen, "Don't Believe Everything You Think— Battling Anxiety," *WHOA That's Good Podcast*, 48:00, hosted by Sadie Robertson, July 21, 2021, https://podcasts.apple.com/us /podcast/dont-believe-everything-you-think-battling-anxiety |/id1433974017?i=1000529547703.

14. Amen, "Don't Believe Everything You Think."

CHAPTER 6: WHAT ARE YOU SHARING AND WHY?

1. Alicia Britt Chole, *Anonymous: Jesus' Hidden Years . . . and Yours* (Nashville: Thomas Nelson, 2006), 27.
2. Christopher Joel Brown, Steven Furtick, Michael Brandon Lake, "Million Little Miracles," Bethel Music Publishing and Maverick City Publishing Worldwide, 2021.
3. Michael Patrick Lynch, "How to See Past Your Own Perspective and Find Truth," TED, video, 14:17, April 2017, https://www .ted.com/talks/michael_patrick_lynch_how_to_see_past_your _own_perspective_and_find_truth.
4. Lynn Okura, "Brené Brown on Shame: 'It Cannot Survive Empathy,'" HuffPost, August 27, 2013, https://www.huffpost .com/entry/brene-brown-shame_n_3807115.
5. Christine Caine, "The Call of God," in *WHOA That's Good Podcast*, 46:00, hosted by Sadie Robertson, December 9, 2020, https://podcasts.apple.com/us/podcast/the-call-of-god /id1433974017?i=1000501806386.
6. Chole, *Anonymous*, 43–44.

CHAPTER 7: ARE YOU FOLLOWING CANCEL CULTURE?

1. Bob Goff, *Everybody Always* (Nashville, TN: Thomas Nelson), 193.
2. Nicole Dudenhoefer, "Is Cancel Culture Effective?" *Pegasus*, University of Central Florida, Fall 2020, https://www.ucf.edu /pegasus/is-cancel-culture-effective/.

CHAPTER 8: DOES GOD STILL LOVE YOU?

1. T. D. Jakes, *Let It Go: Forgive So You Can Be Forgiven* (New York: Simon and Schuster, 2012), 33.

CHAPTER 9: ARE YOU FOLLOWING YOUR TRUTH OR THE TRUTH?

1. John Collins, "Mr. Collins's Sermon," in *Farewell Sermons of Some of the Most Eminent of the Nonconformist Ministers* (London: Gale and Fenner, 1816), 331.

2. "What's on the Minds of America's Pastors," State of the Church 2020, Barna, February 3, 2020, https://www.barna.com/research/whats_on_mind_americas_pastors/.

3. Brian Dodd, "Live Blog from Passion 2021: 35 Leadership Quotes and Lessons from Matt Chandler," Brian Dodd on Leadership, December 31, 2020, https://briandoddonleadership.com/2020/12/31/live-blog-from-passion-2021-35-leadership-quotes-and-lessons-from-matt-chandler/.

YES OR NO?

1. Ideas borrowed from Fresh Life Church's website and used with permission: "How to Know God?" Fresh Life Church, http://www.freshlife.church/knowgod/.

about the author

SADIE ROBERTSON HUFF IS A NEW YORK TIMES bestselling author, speaker, influencer, and founder of Live Original. Communicating as a sister and friend, Sadie is on a mission to reach the world with the message of Christ. The host of the popular podcast *Whoa, That's Good*, which launched in 2018, she continues to top charts and minister to millions of listeners as she engages with current leaders, asking them to answer one question: "What is the best advice you have ever been given?" *Live Original*, Sadie's blog, features encouraging and transparent messages from her and her closest friends, and she is also founder of the online community and app *LO Sister*, which are designed to cultivate sisterhood through Bible studies and workshops. Sadie, her husband, Christian, and their daughter reside in Louisiana.